Miracle Man

*A Novel about God, Prayer
and the Unexpected in Life*

Miracle Man

*A Novel about God, Prayer
and the Unexpected in Life*

Bill McConnell

Wasteland Press

Shelbyville, KY USA
www.wastelandpress.net

Miracle Man:
A Novel about God, Prayer and the Unexpected in Life
by Bill McConnell

First Printing — January 2015
ISBN: 978-1-68111-010-3

Printed in the U.S.A.

0   1   2   3   4   5

For Patricia, who has prayed for me for over forty years.

Prologue

John sat in his car for a few minutes before starting the engine. It was just before six in the morning. The hospital parking lot was still. Sunlight was just beginning to show over the mountains, bringing with it a promise of heat later in the day. Though he had managed a few hours' sleep in the chapel, he was exhausted, both physically and emotionally. The drive home would take him around forty minutes, and what waited there would tax him as much as what he had been through in the last few hours.

His ten years of pastoring included many crises. People turned to him when life fell apart, not only for spiritual comfort, but to help with the practical details that surround tragedies in life. For the last several hours he had tried to give both, and as he sat in his car he was certain he had failed. His words brought no comfort and his actions were misinterpreted. Now he had to confront the biggest challenge of the morning: the one that waited for him at home.

Words were his business, but he had no idea what he was going to say. Standing before his people every week in church, he spoke words that he trusted brought hope, comfort, instruction, encouragement and guidance. John had spoken at weddings, funerals, schools, conferences and conventions. He had never been at a loss for words. Even in situations where he had no time to prepare, and that required tact and grace, he was usually able to find the right words to say.

But he had never been in a situation like this before, and try as he might, he could not think how to say what needed to be said. He and Sharon had planned this Saturday night to be a time of fun and entertainment. Instead, he spent the night at the hospital with people he had never met. He tried to make sense of what happened, not only for them, but for him. Yet there wasn't any sense to this tragedy- certainly none that he could see at the moment. John would have normally prayed by now, asking God for wisdom and strength. But for reasons he was well aware of, he could not bring himself to pray. At least not yet.

Part One

1

Tuesday 9.00 am

John had been slowly working his way through the book of Luke for most of the summer, taking his time, trying to look past what was familiar and find truths that were new to him. He had read the book many times before, but this time he was looking for things that lay below the surface. His familiarity with the Bible was such that he read slowly, sometimes out loud, to find the meaning he was looking for.

He usually did his reading in his office at the church. No one else came in until after 9, so he had at least an hour to start his day by reading and then praying for a time. The time he spent in prayer was governed by a notebook he kept on his desk, a notebook whose pages were dominated by the names of people, most of whom went to his church.

Well, it wasn't really his church. He had started it ten years previously and was the only pastor the church had known. John thought of it as his church, but not in a possessive way. He had just enough humility to know that God had blessed his efforts, and just enough pride to know that it was his gifts and personality that enabled the church have grown large enough to now be looking for an associate pastor. The search was beginning in earnest as he had his first interview later in the afternoon.

The interview, however, was not on his mind so he closed his Bible and reached for the notebook he used to keep track of his prayers. As he opened it he looked at the pages filled with names and requests he had written over the years. John was a disciplined person, a quality which had served him well as a pastor. Much of his life was in the notebook, the names of people who entered and exited his life.

There were currently seven people on his list, most in some type of difficulty. Some of them he was seeing on a regular basis, some of them only occasionally, and one that he saw every day. As he looked over the list he could see the people he was going to pray for in his mind, and knew what most of them were doing at that moment. Some would already be at work, some would still be at home, one was in the hospital and one was overseas serving in the military. When he prayed he tried to avoid being repetitive, after all he was talking to God, and though he would not describe himself as having a great amount of faith, he believed that God wanted him to pray for these people. So he prayed.

First, he prayed for a man who was in the hospital. He was the husband of a woman who had been attending the church for nearly five years. He was not a Christian, though he occasionally attended church with his family, usually at Easter and Christmas. Six months ago the man developed brain cancer and for the last three weeks had been in the hospital. His prognosis was not good, and though John had been to see him a few times, he still showed no interest in spiritual things. He seemed resigned to his fate and never complained when John visited.

It was his wife who was having difficulty. They had two young children and she understood what it meant if he died without believing. She was seeing John every week to help with her anxiety about her husband's physical and spiritual condition, but was finding little relief. He prayed for her next.

There were three people on the list that he was also meeting with on a regular basis. John did not like to use the term counseling; he preferred to think of himself as a good listener who would help people find hope and encouragement in whatever situation they were in. He had come to realize through years of talking to people in difficult situations that what they needed most was someone to walk with them through their difficulties. John seldom gave direct advice because so few seemed to take it. He would pray for them, he would ask lots of questions and when asked, would say what he might do in their situation. Two or three times a year he would take a break from dealing with people in that type of setting. He found that if he didn't, he would drown in their sorrows and would not be able to listen or help at all.

The next name was Robert, his mentor, a man who retired from the ministry a few years earlier due to ill health. He met Robert at a pastor's conference several years earlier and sought his advice several times regarding specific issues at the church. He was such a help that they started meeting every week. Robert lived about an hour away, and they met at a diner for breakfast halfway from their respective homes. Robert would not tell John what was ailing him, he would wave his hand and say doctors always suspected the worst and move the conversation in another direction.

He always prayed for her last, though it was getting harder to bring the same request to God nearly every day. John was beginning to think he had already received an answer to his prayer, and he should move on. Yet he could not bring himself to stop, not yet anyway. For six years he had been asking God the same thing, and there had been no movement, no change, and no response. He knew that "no" was an answer, but every time he had that thought, his mind went to verses in the Bible that assured him whatever he asked for he would receive. He was tired of getting into that loop, and just wanted the matter settled so he could move on with his life.

When he was done, he went back to the beginning of the notebook and began to look at the pages covered with names and requests. He did not realize it, but he was looking for something big, something that would border on the miraculous. An answer to a specific request that he could point to and say, "Look, God did this for me". He saw things here and there he would consider answers, but nothing jumped out at him as he turned the pages. Pages that now covered many years.

Though Susan only lived a few miles away, she was usually late. He saw her enter the outer office through the glass in his door, and then looked at the clock on his wall. Late, but not as bad as some days.

In many ways, Susan was the typical church secretary. She answered the phones, reminded the pastor of his appointments, made phone calls to church members to advise them of meetings or responsibilities upcoming and had a tendency to gossip, though she would not think of it that way. She knew who the pastor was counseling, what was happening in board meetings (her husband was on the board), who was sick and whose marriage was in trouble. She was the first person the pastor hired when they moved into their new building seven years ago. She never missed a day of work, thinking that the church revolved around her position as gatekeeper.

While the church met at a high school for its first four years, John had worked at home. When the church had grown enough to raise money for a building (which they expanded twice in the last six years) he knew he would need a secretary to handle the increased volume of phone traffic and operational duties that came with a building.

He asked Robert what he should look for in a secretary. His only advice had been, "Hire someone that you won't be tempted to sleep with." He didn't ask him if that came from personal experience, but over the years he knew it was good advice. He personally knew seven men who left the ministry because they slept with someone on their staff. Susan and her husband had been going to the church since its inception and she was old enough to be his mother. She had not worked before she became the church secretary, but grew into the position over the years as the church increased in size.

She knocked lightly on his door and then opened it slightly to announce her presence. He appreciated her because he could ask her about any person in the church and she always seemed to know what was happening in their life. How she knew, he could not guess, though he could see from the phone in his office that she spent a lot of time on outgoing calls. Because she was efficient and had an upbeat personality that gave a good first impression, he kept her on as the church grew, though she had difficulty with anything involving a computer.

"Good morning pastor, anything unusual this morning," she said.

He had stopped asking her to use his first name years ago, and she was one of the few people in the church who called him "pastor". Because the church was generally informal, and most of the members were young and had no previous church background, they called him by his first name.

"Not yet, but the day isn't over," he replied. This was how they usually started the day, and though it was a cliché, there was a lot of truth behind his remark. It seemed several times a year something happened out of the blue that thrust the church into crisis mode. In the last year two couples were involved in sexual sin that exploded suddenly into the life of the church. John was still trying to put one couple back together, the other couple had divorced and now neither attended the church. With over 250 people attending, he knew that at any given moment some type of crisis was probably brewing.

"Will you call the young man who is applying for associate and remind him of our appointment this afternoon?" John asked.

"Yes, right away" she responded. Then she added, "What's your impression of him from talking to him on the phone?"

Always fishing, John thought. He knew whatever he said might be passed on to the next person she spoke to, so he replied,

"Hard to tell from just talking with him on the phone. I'll know more after I meet with him this afternoon."

She nodded and closed the door behind her as she left. He could see the outgoing phone line light up, and he looked again at the resume on his desk.

Most churches would have hired another staff member a few years previously, but John wanted to develop leaders in the church. If it had been up to him, he would have put off hiring someone longer, but his board was concerned that he was working too much. They were fearful he might burnout if he remained the only paid pastor. He agreed to their wishes, but only on the condition that he determine the duties and responsibilities of the new hire. What they didn't know, and what he didn't tell them, was that he liked working long hours. What else was he going to do?

John wanted someone to begin a process of assimilating people into the mainstream life of the church, something he tried, but unsuccessfully. The church had been growing steadily for several years, but most people still only attended Sunday morning. What he wanted was someone to begin a deliberate small group ministry, train leaders, find material and then convince people to join the groups. Robert told him he could not do everything, that if he wanted it to happen, he would have to hire someone to oversee and manage the program. It was the advice Robert gave him that brought him to the appointment later that day.

He reached for the resume, but his hand was again drawn to the notebook on his desk that held his prayer requests. John opened it and slowly turned the pages, looking one more time at the names and requests filling the pages. When he reached the last page, by the last name he put a question mark and the phrase, "what to do."

John began to write questions on a legal pad he wanted to ask the young man who was coming in that afternoon. He had read and reread the resume, and called a few of the man's references. He paid for a complete background check and had not found anything disturbing. The church received over one hundred responses to its advertisement for an associate on a prominent Christian website. John selected ten names to begin with, an indication that he was going to be thorough in his search. Robert shared with him horror stories of staff he had hired over his years in ministry, and gave John some practical advice on how to conduct an interview with a potential hire. When he had written enough questions to get him started, he put the questions in a folder with the resume and left them on his desk. He had an appointment at ten, and he did not want to be late.

2

Tuesday 10.00 am

He pulled into the parking lot of the medical center and saw she was already there. He purposely avoided parking next to her so she could walk alone to her car if needed. This would most likely be their last appointment, unless the doctor had something new to offer. John explored the Internet for hours on end to become familiar with their dilemma, and knew they were drawing to the end of a long and painful journey. John loved his wife, but he was beginning to think they had entered a new phase in their relationship, one that he called "the new normal". As a pastor, he knew he could help, but not fix people. As a husband, he tried to find the right words that would help them in their situation. He had failed.

Sharon was sitting in a chair across from the receptionist reading a magazine. He could tell by how she was turning the pages that she was killing time and not absorbing anything. When he opened the door to the office she had momentarily looked up to see who was entering, then went back to flipping the pages of the magazine. He sat next to her and said,

"How long have you been here?"

"Not long."

"Busy day at work"?

She sat the magazine on her lap, turned and said,

"Small talk? Really?"

It wasn't like her to be sarcastic. Sharon was usually a model of self-control, carefully measuring her words before she spoke. She was always looking out for John; anticipating his needs, helping out at church whenever needed and not complaining at the long hours he worked. If she had one fault, it was that she was too together, though most people would not consider that a fault. It was rare that she let her feelings show; he guessed that waiting for the doctor was causing her discomfort that showed in her remark. He could ask her how she was feeling, but he knew she would say everything was fine, don't worry about me.

But he did worry about her. He wouldn't say they had drifted apart over the years as much they had become a partnership, with their roles clearly defined. She had never been a demonstrative person, but over time she seemed to have retreated further into herself. He could not find fault with anything she did, and over the years he knew that he had compensated by working longer and longer hours. He understood on some level he was trying to find what he was missing with her in his work. In that too, he had failed.

They both knew what the doctor was going to tell them. This appointment was the end of a journey that began six years ago. They were so much younger then, he thought. Four years into their marriage and they both knew it was time to get professional help. At first, they didn't care about whose fault it was, they only wanted a solution. Like most people, their faith in modern medicine was implicit, and they expected an answer would be found. They put their faith in doctors, and now it was a doctor who was going to tell them that faith was misplaced. It would turn out it was no one's fault, just something that could not be explained.

It wasn't as if they left God out of the picture. They prayed and trusted and waited. They told each other God had a purpose and that He was in charge. As the years passed they knew, though they would not say, they were on a fool's errand and nothing was going to change.

It was hardest on Sharon. At times he felt like he was a bystander, watching from the outside as she became the object of tests, procedures, injections and whatever else the doctors thought she needed. And it was all expensive. For several years it seemed that her entire income as a paralegal went to pay for treatments not covered by their insurance. His parents, who were rich, offered to help, but she wouldn't hear of it. She bore it all very stoically and seldom showed any emotion. If she was feeling distress or disappointment from what they were going through, she wasn't showing it. John did not know how to help, if she even needed any help. Robert told him that the best thing he could do for her was to just be there, and give her time to find her way.

There was one last option open to them, but Sharon wouldn't discuss it. He tried on any number of occasions; the last time he brought the subject up she had not spoken to him for three days. Once, at a church event, a woman innocently brought up the idea and was politely told by Sharon to mind her own business. It wasn't as if their marriage was falling apart, but it wasn't what he expected, and that loss of expectation left him with wounds that would not heal.

The door to the exam rooms opened and the nurse nodded at them. His wife got up and moved purposely while he waited for a moment. He tried to imagine what life was going to be like from now on. Maybe now that it was over they could find some kind of place that included a measure of joy and happiness. But he doubted it, and as he continued to think she turned to him and said,

"Are you coming?"

He managed a smile he did not feel and walked through the door to the conference room where the doctor was waiting.

3

Tuesday 12.00 pm

H e wasn't the only one with an appointment later that day. Sharon had been meeting with a counselor weekly for over two years. John had suggested that it might help having someone to talk with on a regular basis, someone who was neutral and had to keep conversations confidential. His hope was a counselor might help her find a way to say things he knew she must be feeling, but was keeping to herself. When she agreed he was mildly surprised, and he hoped for the best. After two years, he stopped hoping and learned not to ask questions about her time with Amy, her counselor. If Amy was helping Sharon, he could not tell, but the fact that she kept going was something, or so he thought.

They always met during lunch time, so she would not have to miss any work. Amy's office was in the same complex as the lawyers Sharon worked for, making for a happy coincidence. Amy knew from their last appointment Sharon was coming from what might be her last doctor's visit, and thought about how she would be feeling. Sharon was usually forthcoming in their sessions, answering every question that Amy asked, but not with answers that gave Amy much of a window into Sharon's life. After two years Amy felt she was still being held at arm's length, and often speculated why Sharon kept coming.

Her counseling practice consisted primarily of people referred to her by local pastors. These people typically needed more time than pastors could give them. Amy sometimes worked with her counselees for months, and some, like Sharon, for years. Amy's husband had been a pastor for several years, so she understood the environment most of her clients came from.

She heard the door open and looked at the clock on her wall. Sharon always arrived on time, not only because she worked in the same building. Amy felt, but had not yet shared with Sharon, that one of the ways she was dealing with her circumstances was to try and control every area of her life, giving her an illusion of normalcy. When Amy tried to poke around in areas of Sharon's life that might be causing her pain she did not yet realize, Sharon resisted and moved the conversation into areas she felt comfortable with. Something was going to give; Amy had seen this before, but when and what it would look like she did not know.

Amy usually knew where she wanted to begin with her clients, but thought today she would try something different. She knew Sharon would be expecting to talk about the visit to the doctor, and would have a ready response, one that would most likely deflect any serious discussion. When Sharon was seated with legs and arms crossed, Amy said,

"Sharon, how is your mom doing?"

Sharon's mother had been ill for some time, though Sharon would never say what exactly was wrong with her. Amy would find out later that Sharon herself did not know.

What Amy really wanted to talk about was Sharon's father, but she knew she could not begin there. Sharon's eyes narrowed for a moment, and then she said,

"My mother is fine. Why do you ask?"

"I know that you've been concerned about her health. When my mother was ill it caused me a lot of worry and stress. Especially since she lived in another state."

"Did she get better?"

"She did, but it took a long time. And I still worry about her."

"What is your worry going to accomplish?"

Amy knew from talking with Sharon for two years how she would respond. Sharon always wanted Amy to know that she was in control; and that weaknesses that other people had did not apply to her.

"I suspect it won't accomplish anything. It's just who I am."

"I know you believe God is big enough to handle your worry. Why don't you let him?"

They had been down this road before, the two of them. Sharon trying to reverse their roles and become Amy's counselor. Amy didn't mind because it gave their time together a different dynamic, a dynamic she didn't have with her other clients.

"You know, there are lots of people in the Bible who found things to worry about. I think I'm in good company."

"You don't think worry is a sin?"

"I think God knows we all struggle with our weaknesses. I don't think a weakness is always a sin. Do you?"

Amy knew Sharon didn't want to admit that she had any weaknesses. In this respect, Sharon took after her father; a minister who had given Sharon the idea Christians should be able to overcome any fear, doubt, sin, weakness or worry. Amy wondered what it was like living in a household where perfection was held out not only as a possibility but a requirement. Amy also thought about what it was like for Sharon's husband, living in the shadow of Sharon's beliefs.

"I know what God wants from me. He wants me to be obedient. He wouldn't ask me to be obedient if it wasn't possible, would he?"

"Have you ever known anyone who lives like that? Without any weaknesses? I haven't met anyone like that."

"But most of the people you deal with are full of problems, aren't they?"

"Yes, they are. That's why they come and see me. They know they have weaknesses, even sins, and are trying to find a way to be happy and fulfilled."

"I don't think that happiness is the same as obedience. Don't you think people who seek after happiness tend to be self-centered?"

"I think it depends on what you're looking for to make you happy. Would you describe yourself as a happy person?"

Amy knew there was no way Sharon would ever describe herself as happy. As Sharon had said, people who looked for happiness were just thinking of themselves, not on how to please God.

Sharon smiled briefly, knowing she was caught. If she said no, she wasn't a happy person, Amy would ask her why. If she said she was happy, she would be admitting she was self-centered. Instead of answering Amy's question, she said,

"I thought you might ask about my visit to the doctor."

4

Tuesday 11 am

John was certainly not happy, and he would have no problem admitting it to anyone who asked. As he drove back to church he knew one part of his life had ended. There would be no more doctor visits, no more new procedures, no more hope held out to them by the medical profession, and probably no more prayers. Their doctor told them that medicine had nothing left to offer. He could not give them reasons, but everything in his arsenal had been tried, there was nothing else. He was sorry, but then every other doctor they dealt with was sorry as well. John was willing to let it go, except for the fact that there was a solution, one that had nothing to do with medicine.

He thought about giving it one more try since they were now officially at a dead end medically speaking. What's the worst that could happen, he thought? He tried to be understanding toward Sharon, but this affected him as well as her, couldn't she see that? Even if he did speak to her, it could not be today. He needed to give her time to get a handle on her feelings. Sharon pretended to take everything in stride, and not react emotionally to the ups and downs of life. After living with her for ten years he could see when she was struggling. When he tried to talk with her during those times, she told him he was wrong, everything was fine; he should help those people in the church who had real problems.

Maybe this wasn't going to affect her like it was affecting him. Maybe she was relieved that she could now get on with her life, knowing what the future was going to look like. Maybe she would try and find something else to do other than shuffle papers for a bunch of rich lawyers. Maybe the problem was with him, he thought. Maybe he should just accept this and move on, not wasting any emotion for something that wasn't going to change. Maybe he should be more like her. Maybe, but then he thought that would be no way to live. He parked his car and walked slowly to his office, trying to gear up for the interview that was just a few hours away.

Susan's office commanded a view of the parking lot, and she saw the young man get out of his car and walk purposefully toward the front door of the church. He was in a suit, something Susan hadn't seen at the church for some time. She waited for him to find his way to the office, and when he entered she smiled and said,

"You must be Edward."

"Yes ma'am. And you must be Susan." He held out his hand to her with a smile, leaning over her desk as she offered hers in greeting.

"Let me tell the pastor you're here, just sit down for a moment."

She got up and knocked lightly on John's door, then opened it and said,

"He's here."

John too had been looking out his window at the parking lot, waiting for Edward to arrive. He wondered again why he scheduled this meeting on the same day as the visit to the doctor, but what was done was done. He knew he was not in the best frame of mind to talk to someone about something as mundane as a job opening in the church, so he took a deep breath and said to Susan,

"Send him in."

Edward was five years removed from seminary and was working at another church as the youth pastor. He was quite successful in that position, and had the glowing recommendation of his current pastor. John knew youth pastors didn't usually last more than five years in that role, most wanted to move on to something more substantial, eventually becoming a senior pastor. John thought how different it would be to be a youth pastor. Most kids had not lived long enough to get depressed; most didn't have to work full time to support themselves; they could not feel the betrayal of adultery or the shame of being divorced; most kids didn't yet suffer from substance abuse or addictions and most kids who went to church had people who loved and cared for them. Plus, kids were always on the verge of leaving and heading out into the real world, making them someone else's responsibility. From where John was sitting, youth ministry didn't look so bad.

"Come on in," John said. He rose and shook Edward's hand then motioned him to a chair in front of his desk.

"Thank you for coming in. How are you today?"

"I'm fine. Thanks for giving me the opportunity to talk to with you about your church."

Edward wasn't nervous at all, and as he sat in the chair he looked around John's office. Like most pastors, John's walls were covered with bookshelves, though John did most of his studying on his computer. Nearly everything he needed to prepare sermons he found online. He could not remember the last time be bought a book, most of those sitting in his bookshelves were purchased when he was much younger.

"I suppose you must read a lot."

"Not as much as I used to. I don't seem to have a lot of free time."

"Maybe I can help you with that," Edward said.

"Well, maybe you can."

John spent the next several minutes going over the history of the church, how it had come to the place where the board, and John, felt that they needed another staff member to start a more purposeful attempt at helping church members grow in their faith. John was under no illusions, he told Edward, that just attending the Sunday service would build their faith. For one thing, John said, his messages were designed to get people into the church, so he spoke broadly and on common themes that resonated with everyone. They tried small groups, but John did not have the time or energy to train leaders, find material, come up with a plan on how to get people in those groups and then monitor them as time went on. John explained that the person he was going to hire would have to develop this ministry from square one.

Edward went on from there and described how he started with a group of 20 high school kids five years ago and now averaged 150 kids on Sundays and sometimes double that number when they had special events. He found and trained leaders, started small groups for the kids on Sunday mornings in place of traditional Sunday school and was now looking for a new challenge. John knew all of that from reading Edwards's resume, and his mind was wandering. He sat up in his seat and interrupted Edward by asking,

"Edward, how do you deal with disappointment?"

"Excuse me?"

"How do you deal with disappointment? You must have experienced disappointment in your life at some point."

"I suppose everyone has experienced some kind of disappointment. What are you looking for exactly?"

Edward was thrown off balance by the question. He prepared for an interview that would highlight his accomplishments and how they would translate into this opportunity.

"I've got a bunch of resumes here telling me what people have done. I want to know how you've learned to deal with life when it doesn't go the way you want."

John did not tell Edward he wanted to know something about him beyond the obvious. Where he went to school, what he believed, what he had done and why he wanted this job. John knew that under normal circumstances he probably would not have asked this question, but the circumstances of John's day had been anything but normal. He might have even had the hope that Edward might offer some words of encouragement or insight, though this thought did not occur to him. When Edward did not immediately respond, John asked him,

"Edward, let me ask it a different way. What do you do when God doesn't answer your prayers?"

Edward's face brightened when John asked him that question. He had written his master's thesis on the Psalms and knew that he could answer John's question due to his familiarity with that book of the Bible.

"Well, if you look at the Psalms, there are many times that different writers ask God why he isn't answering their prayers or doing what they want. They have doubts, sometimes they get depressed, and sometimes they even question their faith."

He was so young, John though. John was only 35, but had ten years' experience listening to the difficulties, doubts and trials of others. He thought he had answered this question for himself, but now he wasn't so sure.

"I know how the writers of the Psalms reacted, what I want to know is how you feel when God doesn't answer your prayers and leaves you in difficulty you can't handle."

Edward was young, but he was not as naïve or innocent as John thought. Edward realized that John was not asking these questions about Edward, but about himself. It came across more in John's body language than in his words. John hadn't been maintaining eye contact with Edward and was instead looking out the window toward the parking lot.

"I guess that I haven't been in a situation like that yet. Have you?"

John turned around in his chair and chastised himself for letting the conversation become about him. He knew he had been affected by the events of the day, but he did not realize until that moment how deeply. He got up from his chair and motioned for Edward to follow him.

"Let me show you around the church."

5

Wednesday 8.00 am

The next morning John was heading down the freeway for his weekly meeting with Robert. He had spent more than two hours with Edward the previous day, and came away favorably impressed. The more time he spent with him, walking around the church and then heading over to Starbucks, the more John thought he and Edward might be able to work together. John knew he should interview at least a few other candidates, but he did not want Edward to get away from him. He knew Edward had at least one other church interested in him, so he wanted to get him before the board as quickly as possible.

John was also going over in his mind how he might bring up, probably for the last time, the issue of adoption. They had not talked about the doctor's visit last night; in fact they really hadn't talked about anything. They circled around each other with small talk about her work and some interesting cases she was working on, and then he watched Monday night football in his study. She was in bed before him, a practice that over the last few years had become a habit. He was sure the issue was settled in her mind, but why she would never say. It didn't seem fair that in a marriage one person could get their way on such a huge decision without giving a reason, but that's where they were. He had no doubt Sharon wanted children. In the early years of their marriage they had planned for children, picking out names and wondering if they would have a boy or girl. Now he wasn't so sure, and in his own mind he had come to the point where he almost didn't care one way or the other. He just wanted to understand.

Robert was already there, sitting at a booth drinking coffee when John pulled into the parking lot. Despite his doctor's advice, Robert always ordered something that was too high in fat, or cholesterol, or calories, or something. Though he managed to lose some weight in the last year, John couldn't figure out how, Robert was still a big man. John slid into the booth and said,

"Did you order for me?"

"It's not much of a challenge since you get the same thing every week."

It was true; John always had oatmeal and an English muffin every time they met. Due to the nature of his job, he liked to find consistency and predictability when he could. There was so much that he either could not control or change that he found comfort in having little things that were always the same.

"I suppose you ordered something that your doctor wouldn't be pleased with."

"If everyone ate like you, doctors would go out of business. I figure I'm doing him a favor. Speaking of doctors how was your visit yesterday? I assume nothing has changed?"

John paused for a moment as the waitress poured him some coffee. It gave him a minute to collect his thoughts and think where to begin.

"No, nothing has changed. We're done with doctors. I can't say I'm sorry about that."

"She still isn't willing to consider the one alternative left to you?"

"As long as we were going to the doctors, I didn't want to bring it up considering what happened the last time." John had told Robert of how Sharon hadn't talked to him for three days when he had brought up the possibility of adoption several years ago.

"You know that the problem isn't adopting. The problem is not having a reason."

"Yes Robert, I know that, but right now I'm stuck. If she wanted to adopt, she could bring it up. It makes me think she never wanted kids in the first place."

"I doubt that. She wouldn't have gone to doctors for years if that was true. There's something else here, but unless she tells you, you're never going to know."

John was glad their food arrived, because it stopped the conversation and gave him the opportunity to bring up another subject.

"I talked with my first candidate yesterday. Nice kid. I might have gotten lucky with the first one."

Just as John thought, Robert ordered an omelet that was smothered in cheese and bacon. Robert took a moment as he carved off a piece for himself and slowly chewed, savoring every bite.

"Are you trying to change the subject on me? That's not how this works, you know."

"Well then, what would you do?"

Robert thought for a minute, continuing to attack the food on his plate. Between bites he said,

"John, there is no way to finesse something like this. You're just going to have to ask her. You deserve to know what she's thinking. Above all, you can't get mad, you can't get upset and you can't question whatever reasons she has. This isn't an argument you're going to win. There's something out there that she knows and you don't. She's either going to tell you or not. If she doesn't tell you, you might be able to figure it out, but maybe not. Can you live with that?"

John was already living without knowing, so the only change would be the finality involved. He thought for a moment, and then said,

"Yeah, I can live with that. If I have to."

They spent the rest of their time together talking about Edward and how John might approach his board. Robert suggested getting Edward before them as soon as possible and coaching him on what he would need to emphasize that would make him an attractive candidate. Robert also suggested John have Edward hang around with him for a few days to make sure they were compatible. When they were done, as usual, they spent a moment praying for each other, and then they headed to the parking lot. Robert was headed home, John to church. In order to avoid thinking about anything for the next half hour, John turned the radio on and listened to music, with the volume as loud as he could stand it.

6

"**H**ow is he doing?"

John waited to ask the question until they had spent a few minutes in small talk. Robin had been coming to see him for several months since her husband was diagnosed with brain cancer. John had visited him several times in the hospital and knew that the man would not be going home. The doctors told him it was terminal, that it would only be a matter of weeks until he died. John asked him about his spiritual condition, and whether he was ready for death, to which he replied, "I guess I'm as ready as I'll ever be."

"He's about the same, but I know that he's not going to come home. They haven't told me that yet, but I can see he's getting weaker."

John had seen this before with doctors and terminally ill patients. They held out hope as long as they could, and then when the end was near they usually gave the family time to prepare for their loved one's death. The doctors were usually more candid with him. Because he was a pastor, doctors knew John understood about confidentiality, and trusted he would not share information he received from the doctors with the family.

"You might be right. How are your kids doing? Do they understand how sick Jerry is?"

There were two children, girls, ages 8 and 6, who were going to lose their father in less than a month.

"They know he's really sick. Kendra asked me if daddy dies will he go to heaven. I told her we should pray for daddy, but I can see this bothers her. It bothers me, too."

Once again John was staring at a situation that begged the question, why isn't God answering my prayer. John knew Jerry wasn't interested in God, never came to church, but was a good husband and father. The last few times John visited Jerry in the hospital he kept the conversation off spiritual things because he sensed it bothered Jerry. John knew Robin had talked with Jerry many times about God, but like John she had gotten nowhere. Early on in their meetings John advised Robin to be sensitive about how she approached Jerry with the gospel so she would not drive him away emotionally.

He also prayed with Robin numerous times for God to heal Jerry. He prayed at his desk nearly every morning for God to heal Jerry. Jerry's kids prayed for their daddy to get better. Doubtless others in the church were praying for Jerry to be healed, yet Jerry was lying in a hospital bed with a brain tumor that was inoperable and on its way to killing him.

"It bothers me too, Robin. I don't know why God sometimes doesn't answer the way we want. I trust him, but I see these verses in the Bible that assure me God will answer my prayers. Yet here we are."

"You once said in a sermon that "no" is just as valid an answer to prayer than "yes". Do you believe that?"

John had two thoughts. The first thought was he was surprised Robin remembered something from a sermon he must have preached long ago. Second, he wasn't sure he believed that anymore.

Before John could answer Robin said,

"I mean, why are those verses in the Bible if God never answers our prayers the way we want?"

"I don't think it's correct to say that God never answers our prayers the way we want. I think there is an element of trusting that God knows what he's doing."

"Has God ever healed anyone you've prayed for? You've been at this church a long time, surely you've prayed for other people to be healed. Has that ever happened?"

John had prayed for many people to be healed over the years, and over the years many people were better after he prayed for them. However, he could not recall an instance where he prayed for someone to be healed that fell into the miraculous category Robin was talking about. He certainly wasn't going to lie to her, so he said,

"No, I can't think of anyone in a situation like Jerry's that I have prayed for who was healed."

He laid it out for her, and he did not know how she was going to respond. He would not have been surprised if she got up from the chair and walked out, never to return to church. What kind of a pastor was it whose prayers could not move the heart of God to heal someone? He could have said that if God always answered our prayers we would become selfish and turn God into a dispenser of candy. He could have said that if God always answered our prayers we would never learn how to have faith. He could have said there is value in disappointment and suffering. He could have said that maybe they just lacked the requisite faith required to move the heart of God, but he didn't believe that either. Robin said to him,

"Well, maybe this will be the first time."

Whether she spoke out of abundance of faith or just to let him have a way out of the conversation, he didn't know. He nodded his head, but it was just a formality, recognition that he heard what she said.

7

John sat in the hospital parking lot getting up the nerve to visit Jerry. He knew this might be his last visit, and he suspected Jerry knew it as well. He was already mentally planning Jerry's funeral service: what he was going to say, how he was going to help Robin get through the grieving period, how the church might support them financially. Jerry had a large life insurance policy through his work, but Robin's parents were both dead. He knew there would be plenty of generous people who would want to help a widow with two small children. He didn't know what he was going to say to Jerry, but he wanted him to know the church would help his family and watch over them. The doctors had put Jerry on more pain medication and he had not been as responsive on John's last visit. John walked through the main entrance of the hospital and made his way to the elevator that led to intensive care. He had been to this hospital many times over the years, but it had been some time since he had someone who was not a Christian, someone he knew on a casual basis, who was going to die. He had visited many people in the hospital referred to him by church members or friends that needed a minister to be with the family in those last hours before death. In those situations John never knew the patient, and was there mainly for the family.

John stepped out of the elevator and turned towards the ICU. He had to pass through the waiting room outside the ICU and saw Robin sitting in a chair with her back to him. She was talking with an older couple that he guessed were Jerry's parents. John stepped back toward the wall so he would not be seen. He could clearly hear their conversation.

"The doctors don't think that Jerry will live much longer. He seems to be getting worse and there really isn't anything they can do except give him pain medication. The medicine they give him for the pain makes him sleep most of the time. About all I can do is pray at this point."

John knew Jerry was an only child and thought this must be especially hard on his parents. Like Jerry, they did not believe in God.

"It seems like we're past the point that prayer will do any good, don't you think?" said Jerry's dad.

It didn't sound to John that the man was being insensitive or questioning Robin's beliefs, it sounded like he was trying to come to terms with the reality of his son's situation.

"It's all I have left. I don't know what God is going to do, but I know that it's not wrong to pray. I think it helps the kids too, to pray for their dad."

"You don't think that you're giving them false hope? Isn't that worse than doing nothing at all?"

Before Robin could answer a nurse came out of the ICU and spoke briefly to her, and then opened the door so they could all go inside the ward. The three of them rose and followed the nurse, who closed the door behind them.

John moved away from the wall, and thought his presence would unnecessarily fill Jerry's room. He headed off toward the chapel to kill some time. The chapel was usually empty, and this time was no exception. He sat in the back row and began to think again about the funeral, but his thoughts drifted back to Robin's words. Maybe this will be the first time, she had said. John had already decided Jerry's fate, and the thought startled him. What was he doing planning the funeral of someone who was not yet dead? John knew intellectually that God could still heal Jerry, but he also knew he really never believed it. He also knew that his belief or lack thereof, was not the reason God would or would not heal Jerry.

He didn't know how to say what he wanted to ask. God certainly knew John wanted Jerry healed. John had prayed to God nearly every day of his adult life, but this time was different. He slowly moved from the pew to his knees, closed his eyes and asked God to have mercy on Jerry and his family by healing the tumor that was killing him. There really wasn't anything else to say, so John rose to his feet, turned, and walked out of the chapel. Instead of heading to Jerry's room, he left the hospital and made his way to his car. The certainty didn't hit him all at once, but grew slowly as he drove to the office. By the time he returned to the church, he knew what was going to happen, but would have one more moment of doubt.

8

John usually led the board meetings. Over the years the board tried different formats, but settled on having John lead them because he knew most everything that was going on in the church. He emailed an agenda to the four other members and encouraged input on what they were going to talk about.

The four board members had served together with John for three years. Wayne was a contractor who had attended the church for seven years. John met him when he needed some work done on his house. Wayne and his wife had never attended any church and were initially skeptical when John asked them to visit. But John's church was not what they expected, and after a year both of them were baptized and became members. As might be expected, Wayne was extremely loyal to John. Michael was Susan's husband, and had been at the church almost from the beginning. They moved into the area after a job transfer and had seen a sign for the church, which was then meeting at the local high school. Because Susan was the church secretary, Michael knew almost everything that happened at the church. Randy came to the church after a bitter divorce several years previously, looking for a place where he could start over. He met his current wife at the church. After John married them, he spent a lot of time helping them come to terms with their past relationships. Like Wayne, Randy was close to John and gave him complete support.

Finally, there was Tim. Tim was the oldest member of the board and was close to retirement. He worked for the city as a mid-level manager in the water department and brought the mind of a civil servant to the board. He was cautious, conservative to a fault and loved dealing with facts and figures. Tim was Michael's best friend and the two of them would often finish each other's sentences.

John tried to keep the meetings to two hours, having learned if they went longer less would actually be accomplished. The board usually spent the first hour on items related to the operation of the church; budgets, the building and anything else that had to do with money. John learned over time that you had to talk about money; it was part of everything the church did and wanted to do. They spent their last hour talking about future events, programs and the needs of various members. They closed with a time of prayer, and that was it until the next meeting, which was usually a month later.

This meeting would be different. Though John sent out an agenda with items that were typical, he decided he would begin by talking with them about Jerry and Robin. When everyone arrived and after they spent some time in small talk, John began.

"I want to vary the format a little and begin by talking about Jerry. I met with Robin this week and we talked about what's happening in their family."

"How is he doing?" asked Michael.

"Not well. I don't think there is anything else the doctors can do. I went to see him yesterday but there was a lot of family so I just spent some time praying in the chapel."

"Can't hurt to pray. How is Robin handling this?" said Tim.

"That's what I wanted to talk about tonight. In my conversation with Robin she asked why God doesn't answer our prayers concerning Jerry. She then asked me some questions that I couldn't answer."

This brought a silence to the room, an awkward pause they all felt. Tim broke the silence when he asked,

"What kind of questions exactly"?

"She wants to know why there are parts of the Bible that say God will answer our prayers, without any conditions." Robin hadn't exactly said it that way, but John was sure that was what she meant. Tim responded,

"There are also parts of the Bible that say we need to pray in line with the will of God, if I remember correctly."

"Yeah, that's true. But I guess she would say she doesn't understand why it might be God's will for her husband to die from a brain tumor that God could heal. Plus the bigger concern for her that Jerry isn't a Christian. If Jerry dies, she knows he's not going to heaven."

"John, everybody dies. There is no getting around that. Some die younger than others, some of us live longer than we probably want to."

"Tim, I don't think the issue for Robin is about abolishing death, if that were possible. It's about God doing something that he said he would do. In this case, answer our prayer for Jerry to be healed."

Michael had been looking through his Bible as the two men spoke. When John was finished he said,

"I have been reading in the Psalms and remember this verse from Ps. 69. It says. 'But as for me, my prayer is to you, O Lord, at an acceptable time O God, in the greatness of your loving kindness; Answer me with Your saving truth.' It seems presumptuous to say to God he has to answer our prayers when and where we want."

John listened as Michael read the verse. It was so typical, he thought, to hear what you wanted to hear. To fit a verse into your view of how God works. To miss what it was saying though the words were right in front of you.

"Michael, did you listen to what you just read? It says that God will answer at an acceptable time. It doesn't say that he won't answer at all. I would say that Jerry's "acceptable time" is running out."

"You can't mean to say that God will answer every prayer we ask?" Randy asked this question with a hint of exasperation, as if the conversation were getting out of control.

"Randy, I don't think that's the issue. I'm struggling with the idea that God doesn't seem to answer any prayers that would involve something miraculous. Something out of the ordinary. Something that we can point to and say, God did this and there is no other explanation."

John was thinking of his notebook. That it contained all of the requests he made over the years and how few of them could actually be considered "miraculous". He continued,

"Guys, you have to give me some grace here. I'm trying to help a woman whose husband is dying, and I find myself at a loss to say something that will bring her any hope or encouragement."

Randy asked John what everyone was thinking,

"What did you tell her?"

"I told her that I didn't know. She also asked me if I'd ever prayed for someone who was ill and then they were healed. I told her that though people I've prayed for have recovered, I have never prayed for someone in Jerry's condition who was healed."

John was trying to bring the group to the place where he was, grappling with a big question that defied an easy answer. This was way out of their comfort zone, and John could see that he had caught them unawares.

"John, if God answered every prayer for healing, people would come to church just for that reason, wouldn't they?"

Michael had a good point, an argument made by others who tried to explain how God works. He also completely missed the point, John thought.

"Michael, you're right, but do you think God never answers this type of prayer?"

John had put emphasis on the word "never", and waited for a response. When none was offered, he said,

"When I talked with Robin I didn't have anything to offer her except to trust God. That didn't seem like much at the time. Especially in view of the verses that talk about God answering our prayers. It still doesn't. You know what she said to me? She said, "There is always a first time"."

Randy spoke again and said, "Shouldn't that be enough? To trust God?"

"Yes, it's always enough for us to trust God, Randy. No matter what the circumstances. But Jesus also said that we should ask him for things so that our joy may be made full. I can't imagine anything that would make Robin more joyful than having her husband healed."

"John, what do you want us to do?" Tim asked.

It was typical of Tim to try and get to a place where he needed to fix something or find a resolution. It was always good to have someone in a group like that, to move the group forward towards achieving stated objectives and goals. But in this case they were not dealing with specific goals or objectives or numbers on a spreadsheet.

"I don't want us to do anything. I just wanted you to know that I have prayed Jerry will be healed and that he will come to believe."

"We all pray for that, John", said Tim, unsure what John meant.

"But I suspect that we don't believe it will happen, do we?" John was not accusing them of anything, and spoke in a manner that conveyed just a touch of sadness.

"Do you mean that you believe Jerry is going to be healed?" Michael asked what everyone was thinking.

John spoke slowly so they would understand what he meant to say.

"I have prayed that God would heal Jerry and open his heart to believe."

Wayne was probably the closest to John in the group, and knew something of John's continuing disappointment in God not answering his own prayers. He said,

"John, how are you going to feel if God doesn't answer this prayer?"

"Like I said, I have prayed God will heal Jerry and that he will become a Christian."

John looked around the room and let the silence speak for him. He was not going to give them anything else to discuss because there was not anything left to say. John was tired of the board, and he included himself, trying to put everything spiritual into a box they could easily wrap and unwrap when needed. Though he might be accused of presuming he knew what God was going to do, he didn't care. John was looking for a demonstration that God would do something that showed that he was there and listening. Answering "no" to every prayer could leave one with the impression that God's default position on answering requests was just that, "no", and that he was not listening or concerned. John did not believe this, but his faith was being stretched thin, and some on the board were wondering where their pastor was spiritually.

9

He didn't usually work on Saturdays, but he had scheduled an interview with another candidate for that afternoon. John had talked with the board about Edward, and though they wanted to meet him, they also wanted John to speak with at least two other men. Since Saturday was the earliest this man could meet, John arranged to meet him at the church just after lunch. That left him the morning to have the conversation he had been putting off all week.

Sharon usually slept in on Saturday, and it wasn't until nearly ten that she came into the kitchen for breakfast. John had been up for several hours, most of them spent thinking how he was going to begin a conversation that only he wanted to have. Finally, he came to the conclusion that since there was no easy way, it probably didn't matter how he brought it up.

"Can I get you some coffee?" he asked.

Sharon had sat down at the kitchen table and begun to turn the pages of the newspaper he had left there for her.

"That would be nice. Thanks."

He sat the cup down next to the paper, and then went back to the sink to pretend to clean dishes left from last night's dinner.

"We haven't talked about the doctor visit. How we're feeling. What we might do next."

So he put it out there, without actually using the word. Sharon put down the paper so she could address him directly.

"I should think that it's obvious. I don't know what you're feeling, but I'm feeling relief. I spent six years being poked and prodded, and now I'm done. And John, there is no next."

"I know that you haven't wanted to discuss any other options. You've never explained why. I would like to understand."

He purposely kept his back to her as he put the few dishes in the sink into the dishwasher. He did not want to appear confrontational, and figured if he did not meet her gaze it would be easier. He was wrong.

"John, did it ever occur to you that God might not want us to have children?"

She spoke in such a way that he knew she was convinced that having children was not in their future.

"No, and I didn't think that it had ever occurred to you until you refused to discuss adoption. It is an alternative, and one that people chose every day. Why isn't it an option for us? That's all I want to know."

The last time he had brought this up, years ago, she didn't get mad. She merely looked at him while shaking her head, and did not speak to him for three days. He got the point. When she answered him there was an edge to her voice.

'What makes you think that we would be good parents? What makes you think that we could raise children that would do what we wanted? That would make us proud? Don't you deal with people all the time who are having problems with their kids?"

Where did this come from, he thought? He turned around from the sink and looked her straight in the eye. He didn't know how to respond, and he wanted her to see the confusion on his face. In all of the people he had talked with over the years who had problems with their children, and there were plenty, no one ever said to him they wished they never had children. He was in over his head, and he knew it.

"I'm sorry. You're probably right. Sometimes I feel like I need to understand or fix everything that's going on in my life. But I forget that this affects you more than me. I won't bring it up again."

"Good. And I'm not something that you need to fix. You and Amy need to understand that."

She left the table and headed back to get ready for her daily visit to the gym. He could not remember the last time she missed a day. He suspected that exercise added something to her life that was missing, but he could not say what. John thought it would take a day or so for things to return to normal, which he could live with. Her words about parenting were still a mystery to him, and made no sense. There were two people who might know what she was talking about, two people he would be sure to talk with in the next week.

10

Monday 9.00 am

They met at a Starbucks close to the church. He did not want to meet near Amy's office because of the chance that Sharon would see them. It was a nice day and John was sitting outside enjoying the sunshine when he saw Amy at the counter ordering her drink. She agreed to meet him but John knew she would not tell him anything she had learned about Sharon in their sessions. John understood this, but also knew he might be able to get some insight by asking her questions of a general nature. When she sat down at the table she said,

"Nice day. It feels good to get outside."

"For me too. Thanks for taking the time to meet with me. You can charge me if you want."

It was a lame attempt at humor, something they both recognized as a way to acknowledge John wanted help from Amy.

"You've sent me enough clients that I think I can let it go this time. Plus, I don't know how much I'm going to be able to help you."

"I understand. I'd like to ask you some questions that might help me in a couple of situations I'm in right now."

"Ask away."

Amy was intrigued to see how John was going to approach what she assumed was going to be a conversation about Sharon. She was mildly surprised when he said,

"Do any of the people that come to you ever talk about prayer? About why God might not be answering their prayers? How that affects them?'

"You want to ask me about prayer? I wasn't expecting that."

"What were you expecting?"

"I think we both know what I was expecting."

She paused for a moment, then continued,

"Most of the people that come to me are trying to deal with something that's causing them pain or hurt or sorrow or grief or worry or anxiety. I'm usually the one bringing up prayer as a way to help them, not the other way around. I would think that in your position people would be coming to you if they had questions like that."

"I had someone come to me recently, and I don't think I've been much help. I can't seem to give a good reason why God won't answer their prayer."

"Can you tell me what this prayer is about?"

"They want to know why God won't answer a prayer that would heal someone they love. Someone who is dying."

"How is this affecting them? Depressed, unable to sleep, anger?"

"Surprisingly enough, they're handling it well. I'm the one that's having some difficulty."

"How?"

"Amy, I'm trying to figure out why God doesn't seem to answer prayers that are big. Or why he waits and waits and waits to answer prayers that I think need to be answered now. I'm not talking about prayers that are selfish, or at least that I think are selfish. I'm talking about prayers that would alleviate suffering and that would fix broken relationships. Prayers that would bring people to Jesus. And would heal their bodies."

John reached behind his chair and took a notebook out of his briefcase. He opened it and began to turn the pages so Amy could see the names and requests.

"I've been keeping notebooks like this for a long time. As I look back I find most of these are unanswered. Some have been, and I'm thankful for that, but most are just sitting there on the page, and I don't quite know what to make of it."

"Why has this become an issue lately? This thought can't just be occurring to you now?"

"I think that as long as I was involved in actually praying for people, I wasn't really looking for answers. I think I might have been praying for the sake of praying. I don't really know. Plus, I was asked if I had ever prayed for anyone who was healed. I had to answer no. Somehow, that doesn't seem right."

"Have you thought to ask God why he hasn't answered your prayers?"

This was a new thought to John, and he smiled when he thought that God might not answer a prayer about why God wasn't answering his prayers.

"Amy, everything I believe about God tells me he loves people. That he wants to have a relationship where we love him back and experience his presence in our lives. He's given us all these assurances in the Bible that he wants to be involved in our lives. Some of that has to do with how he responds to our requests to him as our father."

"You haven't answered my question."

"Why would I ask God why he isn't answering my prayers when it says in the Bible that he will?"

"It says in the Bible God will answer all of your prayers? The way you want him to?"

"You sound just like my board. They kept trying to give God an excuse for not answering prayers instead of why he does answer prayers. I guess it comes down to the fact that God seems to say "No" an awful lot more than he says "Yes". That doesn't make sense to me."

"It seems to me a prayer that asks God why he doesn't do what you want is one that he might answer."

"I'm not being selfish here, Amy. I don't want God to do anything for me. I would like him to do something for someone else that would bring good to others. It has nothing to do with me."

Amy knew this had everything to do with John; he just did not realize it at that moment. She knew that though John was not aware of it, he had been struggling with why God hadn't answered one specific prayer in his own life for many years.

"You know that you're not the only one who has struggled with these questions. Others have found answers that have satisfied them. Maybe there isn't an answer that will satisfy you. Can you live with that?"

It was the second time that week he had been asked if he could live with a situation he did not understand. For the moment, he was living with it, he thought. He didn't think this would be a rock that could break his faith, but he had to admit he was living with a vague feeling of unease.

"Yeah, I can live with it. But I've had to live with a few things that I don't understand, as you know."

"It's not necessarily a bad thing to live with issues you can't understand or problems you can't seem to fix. Most of the people that come to me leave with the same difficulties they had when they first walked through my door. They find a way to live with themselves, but find they can't fix the person or situation that brought them to me in the first place. I'm not sure we're meant to understand everything about the way God works or who he is. If we did it wouldn't leave much room for faith, would it?"

John wasn't quite ready to agree with Amy, though he understood what she was saying.

"We're not talking about faith here, Amy. We're talking about words on a page that God wrote and wants us to live by. Those words say God will answer our prayers."

"Do you think that if you had more faith God would have answered your prayers?"

John was getting tired answering Amy's questions. He knew this was how counselors operated, using questions to get their clients to come to grips with what they believed and how they felt about whatever their specific problem was.

"Do I believe that God could heal this person? Sure. I believe that God can do anything. I know that in my head, but how does that translate into walking into a hospital room and telling someone they're going to be healed? How did Peter know he could heal the lame man in Acts? How did Paul know he could heal people? Did God tell them? Did they have more faith than me? How would I know if God was telling me someone was going to be healed? Is me sitting around and waiting to see how God is going to answer any kind of a demonstration of faith?"

John did not tell Amy about praying in the chapel for Jerry to be healed. The certainty was still there, growing in his mind and heart, but because Jerry was still lying in a hospital he was wavering.

Amy knew this part of the conversation had gone about as far as it could. She couldn't answer his questions, and he knew it. She also knew John had at least one other topic he wanted to discuss.

"I think you know that my answer to all of those questions is, I don't know. Is there anything else you wanted to talk about in a more general way?"

"Is this how you leave your clients? With a bunch of questions that don't have any answers? Going out the same way they came in?"

John said this with a smile and knew that if they continued their conversation they were just going to get in a circle they would not be able to find their way out of.

"Some people find getting their questions out in the open gives them some relief, at least in the short run. Those who don't usually have their emotions get out of control at some point. I hope that doesn't happen to you. You also haven't answered my question. Is there anything else you want to talk about?"

John took a sip of coffee just to give himself a chance to move from one difficult subject to another. He knew he would have to talk around it and hoped he could get some insight into Sharon in that manner.

"Have you ever known someone who didn't want to have children because they thought they might be a lousy parent?"

They both knew John was talking about Sharon, but like John this was completely new to Amy. In their time together Sharon had never talked about not wanting children. She talked at length about all the steps she was taking so she could have children, but never about how she thought she might be a bad parent. Amy thought she knew, however, where this was coming from. Did John?

"No. I've never heard that. I've dealt with lots of people whose children have caused them pain and sleepless nights. But I've never had anyone say they wish their kids had never been born. Have you ever had anyone tell you that?"

"Just one."

"Do you have any idea why someone would say such a thing?"

"I think so. And now that I think about it, it might explain some other behavior that I've observed over the years."

"Like?"

"The constant need to be physically fit, for one. Being always in control of your emotions. Not admitting to any kind of weakness. I used to think that these were signs of an organized, disciplined, even spiritual life. Now I'm not so sure."

When John met Sharon years ago in college, one of the things that attracted him to her was her spiritual devotion and level of commitment. She spent time every day reading the Bible, praying and lead two women's Bible studies on campus. John thought at the time this marked her out as someone who was truly devoted to God and wanted to serve Him. Her relationship with John took a more serious turn when he told her he wanted to go into the ministry. Besides her good looks, which brought interest from other men on campus, John believed he found someone who wanted to follow God for the same reasons he did. Now he was beginning to think Sharon's behavior may have a completely different explanation.

"Most of us would love to be that kind of person. What makes you think these things are in any way negative?"

"For one thing, who can keep in control of their emotions all the time? It's not natural and it's certainly not the norm for most of us. But for some people I think it's a point of pride that they can control themselves in a way that others can't. Then when you introduce God into the picture, it's like this is what God wants, for us to be completely in control of our lives."

This was the first time John was expressing these thoughts, and he knew he wasn't saying it the way he wanted. He hoped Amy understood what he was driving at. She did. Amy responded by saying,

"I've known people like this. They don't often make it to my office because they feel they have life figured out. Coming to a counselor would certainly be an admission of weakness, so they usually stay away."

"So why would a person like this let you poke around in their lives if they feel there isn't anything to find?"

"For that exact reason. To be validated. And sometimes to try and show the counselor that they're smarter and more together than the counselor is. In my case, it's not that hard to do."

'Where would this person get the idea that you have to be perfect? That you need to be better than everyone else?"

"There are two places I've seen this happen. I'm sad to say that a lot of churches teach this, though they won't admit it. What drove my husband out of the ministry were the expectations people had of him. He was never going to be what they wanted, so he quit. Probably saved our marriage. A lot of pastors do the same thing; push expectations on their congregations they will never personally meet. And the worst thing is they imply that the better they act the happier God is with them. It's a treadmill you can stay on your entire life. Trying to be as good as you can so God will love you more and realizing you can never be as good as he wants."

As Amy was talking, John was trying to think if he ever gave that impression to his church, that the better they behaved the happier God was with them. He didn't think so, but he knew pastors that probably veered in that direction.

"Where's the second place this happens?" John asked.

"I think you know the answer to that, don't you?"

John thought for a moment, and then said,

"Yeah, I think I do."

There was one more question Amy wanted to ask John. One so obvious she was surprised he had not brought it up.

"One last thing. Here's something I don't understand. Why would a person who didn't want kids because they thought they would be a lousy parent go through years of treatments to try and get pregnant?"

John thought for a moment, and then said,

"I have no idea. And I'm afraid to ask."

11

Tuesday 8.00 am

Sharon's father lived about forty five minutes away in the city where John and Sharon attended college. He pastored a church there for almost thirty years and had recently retired. John thought when he became a pastor it would perhaps bring the two men closer, but he was wrong. Sharon's father tolerated John, but just barely. He had the distinct feeling her father thought she could have done better, but he guessed many fathers shared that same thought.

They met at a restaurant, and it didn't surprise John that Mr. Banks was wearing a suit. John knew it was a subtle statement making the point that John never wore a suit when he preached and certainly not when he was in the office. The suit, combined with Mr. Banks tall, lean frame and nearly bald head, make him look like an undertaker. Sharon's father had visited John's church a few times over the years and wasn't shy about offering comments, comments that were along the lines of: Why don't you preach through Bible books (John typically preached on topics and looked for verses that supported that topic), Why do you use so much video (John used video clips to not only support his messages but to set the tone for the service), Why don't you have an altar call? (John never asked for people to come forward after a message), and finally, Why is the music so loud? (John's church had a band that prominently featured three electric guitars).

John could have dealt with his father-in-law's comments if he felt they were mostly generational, but John knew the man had a distrust of anything outside his own experience. This wasn't unusual. John had known a few other older ministers who could not adjust to anything "contemporary". What was unusual was the man had almost no interest in seeing his daughter. His only other child, a son, lived across the country and seemed to be content to never see his father. John couldn't remember the last time Sharon's family was all together. It had to be at least eight years. Mr. Banks never visited, he seldom called, and seemed content to let his daughter live a short distance away and not have any kind of relationship,

What was even more baffling was Sharon's mother followed the same pattern. While John had difficulty being around the father, he genuinely liked the mother. She was kind, easy to talk with and seemed to have accepted John into the family. John suspected there was some kind of unspoken communication between Sharon's father and mother that kept them from seeing their daughter. At least John hoped it was unspoken. The thought of Sharon's father telling his wife that she could not talk to her daughter saddened him, though he would not put it past the man.

John walked into the restaurant and found him sitting at a booth looking over the menu. Before John sat down he offered his hand and said,

"Mr. Banks, nice to see you. How are you?"

Though he had known the man for over a decade, he could not bring himself to call him anything other than "Mr. Banks".

"I'm fine. Sit down. What did you want to see me about?"

John knew Mr. Banks would be curious why John wanted to see him; this was the first time that John initiated a meeting with him in memory. John was somewhat surprised he agreed to see him, especially since John had given no reason why he wanted to meet.

John didn't know any easy way to begin a conversation with Sharon's father. He couldn't remember the last time he had talked to him, and he was sure they had never met together without anyone else present. John thought it would be best to just get on with it.

"I wanted to talk with you about something personal, if that's okay. But I'd like to know how your wife is doing. And your son."

"I don't know why you would want to talk with me about something personal. I imagine you must have other people you could speak with."

Before John could answer a waitress stopped and asked if John would like some coffee, and were they ready to order. John answered,

"I'll have some coffee, and oatmeal with an English muffin. Thanks."

"Nothing for me, just the coffee."

It didn't escape John that Mr. Banks refused to talk about his family, but that was not going to be possible. As soon as the waitress left John said,

"I do have some friends that I speak with regularly about my life, but in this case I need to talk with you. It's about Sharon."

Mr. Banks sat up straight and leaned slightly across the table.

"What about Sharon?"

"You know that we've been trying to have a child for many years. It seems we have come to a dead end. There is one option open to us, but she won't consider it."

"Maybe you should consider the fact that God may not want you to have children. It is God who opens and closes the womb. If God wanted you to have children, you would have children."

Because John knew how Mr. Banks viewed the world, and how he felt God worked in people's lives, this remark did not offend him. Mr. Banks lived in a world that was generally black and white, good versus evil and right versus wrong, with few if any shades of grey.

"Mr. Banks, when I get sick I go to the doctor because something is wrong with my body. I'll bet you do the same. I don't think it's much different to try and get medical help if there might be a medical reason my wife can't conceive."

John spoke calmly and without emotion. He had much more he wanted to say to Mr. Banks and he didn't want the conversation to end abruptly. He continued,

"The one option open to us is adoption, and she has been adamantly opposed to it. But she would never give me a reason. Until recently, when she told me she felt she couldn't be a good parent. That she didn't feel she could raise children who would make her proud. Do you have any idea why she might say something like that?"

"None whatsoever. Do you?"

"I think I might, but I won't know for sure unless you can answer some questions for me?"

"What kind of questions?"

Mr. Banks was from a generation that seldom talked about their personal lives. To get him to talk about his children and how they were raised, what he expected of them, how he talked to them; it would be close to a miracle if he let John ask him about things that he probably never talked about with anyone else. John at this point had nothing to lose. He began by asking something he thought was harmless.

"Was Sharon a happy child?"

"Why does that matter now? She's been an adult for many years."

"I've been married to her for over ten years and though she seems to be well adjusted, I wouldn't describe her as happy. I wonder if she's always been like this."

"What you think is happiness she might call being obedient. She might find more satisfaction in life in doing what is right than being happy, whatever that is."

"She was an obedient child?"

"Both her and her brother."

"What do you attribute that to?"

With the conversation headed in a direction where Mr. Banks could talk about his views on childrearing and how his children always behaved correctly, he became more expansive.

"I expected them to do what I asked. My belief is that if the Bible tells us to do something, then God expects that we can do it. I never asked them to do anything that wasn't in the Bible."

"They never questioned anything? They didn't ever try to change your mind on something that you told them they couldn't do?"

"I think they knew that what I expected of them was what God expected of them. They knew what the consequences would be."

John knew it was futile to tell Mr. Banks that many people disobey God knowing full well what the consequences would be. John didn't have to ask him what the consequences would have been had his children disobeyed.

"How did you decide what was right and what was wrong in what some would call the grey areas of life? Things like music, movies, going to school dances, clothes, things like that. Did your kids ever try and push the envelope in any of those areas?"

John knew that Sharon had what some would call a "sheltered childhood". She went to Christian schools and the list of things she was not allowed to do was quite extensive. When John first met Sharon, in her second year at a Christian college, she had never been to a movie, never been to a school dance and had never been on a date. Looking back, John could see the long shadow of her father hovering over her.

"I don't think there are as many grey areas as you think there are. I know that your upbringing was much different than Sharon's, and to tell you the truth I'm surprised she married you."

Mr. Banks wasn't telling John anything he didn't already know, though Mr. Banks had never said it so clearly. John didn't tell his father-in-law that Sharon kept the same set of rules she had when she lived with him. She didn't like to go to movies, she seldom watched anything on television that wasn't educational and had no interest in anything cultural. She limited her world to work, church and some form of exercise.

"Well, to be honest with you, I wonder sometimes why she married me too. But then I wonder sometimes why she wanted to be married at all. She's always been very self-sufficient. Would you have preferred she married someone else or not even married at all?"

"I always assumed she would get married, for most people that's God's plan. I had my doubts you would be the best person for her, but at least she married a minister."

It was beginning to become clear to John that Sharon married him in part because of his desire to become a pastor. He wasn't ready to think she married him because her father was a minister, but there was that possibility. Because they were so different, he wondered if on some level she was unaware of she might have married him as an act of defiance to her father. Then he thought there probably wasn't anyone her father would have approved of.

"And you still have your doubts?"

"What does it matter now?" He paused for a moment as a new thought occurred to him, and then he said,

"You're not going to get divorced, are you?"

"Why would you say that? I don't think I've even suggested that, have I?"

"Because that seems to be what married people do today when they're unhappy, isn't it?"

"Mr. Banks, did I ever say I was unhappy being married to Sharon? I'm trying to understand her so I can help her find some happiness, which I think you would also want as her father."

Mr. Banks turned his head and began looking around the restaurant for their waitress. When he finally saw her he raised his hand to get her attention. Without looking at John he said,

"I'll bet they forgot about your order. It shouldn't take this long." He was getting visibly upset and John guessed he had pushed Mr. Banks too far.

"It's okay, Mr. Banks, I'm sure it's almost ready. Don't worry about it."

John immediately realized he said the wrong thing. Mr. Banks turned to him and said,

"I'm not worried about anything. I just expected they would have better service. I don't think it's too much to ask to get your order in an expeditious manner."

When the waitress arrived at their table she went to fill Mr. Banks coffee cup. He stopped her by putting his hand over the top. Before he could speak to her John smiled and said,

"I was wondering where my oatmeal was. If my stomach growls any louder it's going to scare away your customers."

"I knew there was an order that should have been up. Let me go find out right now. I'll be right back."

Mr. Banks followed her with his eyes, upset he did not get a chance to take charge of the situation. John knew he wasn't going to get any more information from him about Sharon, but he did have one more question he wanted to ask.

"Mr. Banks, I have one more question I'd like to ask you. It's kind of a theological question. Why do you think God doesn't always answer our prayers?"

Mr. Banks turned to John and narrowed his eyes, and if he was taken aback by the sudden change of direction in the conversation he did not show it.

"I don't know about you, but God always answers my prayers."

John expected this type of answer, and responded,

"By that you mean that when God answers "no" you're just as satisfied as when he says "yes" ".

"By that I mean God knows exactly what's best for me. If God answered every prayer "yes" I would hate to think what type of person I would become."

"You're saying by answering "no" God is saving us from ourselves?"

"In a manner of speaking, yes. But then I wouldn't expect you to understand. Your generation of ministers seems to be very presumptuous with God."

The waitress returned with John's food and placed it in front of him. John looked down and realized he had no desire to eat. He kept looking at the oatmeal and the English muffin without speaking; not wanting to extend the conversation any longer and wishing Mr. Banks would just go away. In this he was rewarded.

"I'll leave you to eat your meal. I need to be going anyway."

With that Mr. Banks rose, took his bill and went to the counter to pay. John followed him with his eyes, taking note that he did not say goodbye, did not leave a tip and did not ask John to greet his daughter.

12

Tuesday 12.30 pm

Later that day John met Robin for lunch at the hospital cafeteria. The meeting with Sharon's father was still on his mind when he saw her sitting at a table waiting for him. John took a deep breath to try and clear his mind and said a short prayer to be able to say the right words. He came up behind her and touched her gently on the shoulder before he sat down across from her.

"How are you doing? How is Jerry today? I came by the other day to see him but it looked like his family was visiting so I thought it best to not intrude."

She had a cup of tea in front of her and he could tell from looking at her face that she had not been getting much sleep.

"I wish I had known you were there. Sometimes I don't know what to say when I'm around his parents. They aren't Christians either and it seems like we all just talk around everything. They mean well but I think they're in denial about Jerry's condition."

John wanted to tell her he probably wouldn't have been much better with them, but instead said,

"How is Jerry's condition? What are the doctors telling you?"

John knew from looking at her face Jerry had not improved and what she was going to say. It was only a few days earlier that John had sat in the chapel and prayed Jerry would be healed. When she told him Jerry was not improving and that the doctors were being more open with her about his condition being terminal, he did not feel doubt or discouraged.

"Do you want to get something to eat?" she said. "You must be hungry."

He was hungry, having left his oatmeal and English muffin uneaten at the restaurant. It struck him that Robin was looking out for him and making sure his immediate need was being met, and that in the midst of her grief and pain was thinking of someone else.

"Yeah, I could eat. I didn't have much of a breakfast. Let's go see what looks good."

John ended up with a sandwich and chips while Robin settled for a premade salad. He doubted she had much of an appetite; in fact it looked to him like she had lost weight since Jerry had been hospitalized. This wasn't uncommon, but it still concerned him, and he said to her as they sat back down,

"How are you doing? You look a little rundown; do you need any help at home? Is there anything the church can do for you? Watch the kids? Bring some more meals?"

A group of ladies from the church had been bringing meals every few days for the last few weeks and some offered to watch the kids if needed.

"John, I have enough food to last for weeks", she said with a smile. Robin was too polite to prevent people from helping, he thought, though he would talk with the lady who was coordinating the effort and have them adjust the frequency.

"What about you Robin? How are you doing?"

He didn't like asking the question twice, but he wanted Robin to talk about what she was feeling and thinking. John really wanted to ask her about some of the things they had talked about in his office, but thought it would be best if she brought that subject into the conversation.

"I'm on a roller coaster most of the time. I try to spend as much time here as possible, but I need to be with the kids, too. There are plenty of people who will watch them, but I know when I'm here they're thinking that daddy is getting ready to die."

"They understand that?"

"Kendra does, and I think she has told Allison that daddy is very sick and may not come home." Kendra was 8 and Allison 6. Robin paused for a moment, looking down at her salad.

John thought back to their time in his office when Robin said the kids were aware that daddy might not go to heaven. Their understanding was most likely based on the fact that because Jerry did not attend church he would not go to heaven. In the kid's experience people who believed in God went to church, and when they died they went to heaven. Robin then looked up and said,

"I think we need to talk about planning a funeral. It's probably best to do it now while I have some energy and emotional stability. I know I'll probably be overwhelmed by details after he dies."

Though she said those words without emotion, she began to tear up and quietly cry, wiping at her eyes with a napkin. John had been with many people in similar situations, and her behavior was typical for someone going through this type of experience. He would usually give the person their moment of grief or sadness, and then try and offer words of consolation or hope. But there wasn't any hope or consolation to offer her, and she knew this. She was surprised, therefore, when he asked,

"Have you thought anymore about what we talked about in my office? About why how God does and doesn't answer prayer. I know you have prayed for Jerry, not only to become a Christian but to be healed."

He doubted she was going to bring it up so he jumped in with both feet, not knowing where he was going to land.

She looked at John and studied his face, trying to see where this question was coming from. Robin knew she had given up thinking Jerry was going to be healed. She wouldn't let herself think about his spiritual condition, the thought was too final and too emotionally draining. If anyone else asked her this question she would have found it much too intrusive and personal. But she trusted John, though she did not understand why he would ask something that he could not answer just a few days ago.

"Are you asking if I'm mad at God? For not healing Jerry?"

"I don't really know what I'm asking. We didn't really seem to resolve anything that day, and I wonder how that's affected you. I know I've spent a lot of time thinking about it. And I would completely understand if you were mad at God. You certainly wouldn't be the first person, and some would say you have a right to be."

John was thinking back to the conversation he overheard in the ICU waiting room. He knew if it had gone on any longer Jerry's parents might have inferred that God was either letting her down or a fable she was leaning on to get through life. He had seen people get angry at God before, usually in the same type of situation. When life's expectations were not being met. He particularly remembered one couple whose teenage son had thrown his life away into drug addiction. They walked away from God when their disappointment overwhelmed them. In his last conversation with them John suggested instead of walking away from God they walk toward him and find comfort in their pain. They didn't take his advice and left the church shortly thereafter.

"John, I don't have the energy to be mad at God right now. And what would it accomplish? Maybe I'll get mad at him later, maybe I won't. Maybe I'll understand all of this later, maybe I won't. You said you've been thinking about all of this. Do you understand any better than you did two days ago?"

Just like he did at breakfast, John poked around at his food without eating it. He knew how he wanted to respond, but he also knew he was heading into waters he had never navigated before. He had been a pastor for ten years and dealt with people in many different situations involving hurt, suffering and loss. He never said to anyone what he wanted to say to Robin. He did not want to be presumptuous with God, as his father-in-law had said, and searched his heart and mind for what to say and how to say it. He thought back to his prayer journal that was sitting on his desk in his office. How the pages were filled with unanswered prayers. With pages that begged for something miraculous, some sign that God would answer a prayer that could only be explained by saying, God did this. Stepping off the cliff he said,

"Robin, I have prayed that God would heal Jerry and that he would become a Christian."

"I know John. We've both prayed that. Many times."

John didn't answer but looked steadily at her, letting the silence speak for itself. Robin's expression slowly changed from questioning to puzzlement as she considered the implication of what she thought he was saying.

"You're not saying that you believe Jerry is going to be healed, are you?"

In a replay of the conversation he had with his board just days before, he said

"I have prayed that God would heal Jerry and he would become a Christian."

Robin now fully understood what John was saying, and thought back to what he had told her in his office. How he did not understand why God would not answer certain prayers. How John had never prayed for anyone who was then healed. How sometimes "no" was just as valid an answer as "yes". She was the one who said maybe this would be the first time John prayed for someone who was then healed, but she was not sure she believed her own words. Or did she? She was confused and mentally thrown into chaos.

"Pastor, don't do this to me. I can't deal with this right now. I know you mean well, but don't give me something to hold onto that's just going to slip away."

It was the first time she had called him "pastor" in years, and he guessed she was taking a step back from him emotionally. He could see she wanted to believe him, but he also knew nothing had changed for Jerry. He was still lying in his bed closer to death today than he was yesterday. John wanted to say something reassuring, but he was prevented when she rose from the table and said,

"I need to go be with my kids."

John was left sitting at the table alone with his thoughts. For the second time that day he left a restaurant without eating his meal, though he did not leave the hospital.

John stood outside Jerry's room talking with the doctor who was in charge of the ICU. John could see through the glass walls Jerry was either sleeping or resting with his eyes closed. The doctor was telling him Jerry was heavily medicated and was in and out of consciousness so John might not be able to talk with him. John asked if he could just sit in the room with Jerry. The doctor had no objection. Then he said,

"You know, he doesn't have a lot of time left."

John nodded his head, though the doctor would misinterpret what John was thinking.

He sat next to the bed and looked at all of the equipment in the room designed to keep Jerry alive and as comfortable as possible. John thought that despite everything the medical profession could invent, devise and throw at disease, everyone was going to die. They may have found ways to extend life, but they couldn't make it last forever. Jerry was going to die, the only variable was when. If Jerry was fifty years older, John doubted he would be praying for him to be healed. Jerry's kids would be older, and perhaps their kids as well would be gathered around their dad and grandfather talking about his life and sharing memories.

Jerry's kids were young, most of his life was still in front of him, and his wife would be a very young widow. John thought about the brain tumor that was robbing Jerry of his life, and tried to picture it slowly strangling his blood vessels. He wondered who would be there when Jerry died, if Robin would be in the room or would they have to call her after it happened. It was usually one of the family members who notified him when someone died, and then John would go to the hospital and help in any way he could. It would not be that way this time. John could not see the exact scenario in his mind, but he knew it was going to be different. After spending close to an hour just sitting with Jerry, who was unconscious the entire time, John was ready to leave. He held Jerry's hand, looked at him and said,

"I'll see you later."

13

Wednesday 8.00 am

For the first time in memory John pulled into the parking lot at the restaurant before his friend. Robert was usually sitting in the same booth when John arrived, but today John was well into his coffee when Robert pulled into the parking lot. John noticed he was moving slowly as he got out of his car and made his way toward the door. When he sat down in the booth he tried to hide the pain he was feeling.

"Moving a little slow today I see. How are you feeling?"

"I'll feel better when I have some coffee. It took me a little longer to get going this morning. I'm fine. Let's not make a big thing about it."

"As you said last week, that's not how this works. I was pretty open with you about what was going on with me. You're obviously in more pain than I've seen you in lately. Has something changed?"

Robert waited for the waitress to serve him some coffee, to which he added milk and sugar. He took a sip and then sat the cup down.

"I might have to miss a few weeks. The doctor has finally found something wrong and wants me to have surgery next week."

John had suspected for some time that Robert was ill. Because he always joked about it John assumed it wasn't anything serious. John had known Robert for many years and noticed that he had slowed down recently, not only physically but also not getting out as much as he had in years past. His wife had died several years earlier and since then Robert's world became even smaller. John thought their breakfast together each week might be the only time he left his house, except to go to church.

"What's wrong?"

"My sedentary lifestyle has finally caught up with my heart. They want to do a triple bypass. Which isn't as big a deal as it sounds, if you can believe that."

"I've known a few guys who've had bypass surgery. They all bounced back pretty fast as I recall."

"I bet they weren't as fat and out of shape as me. Right?"

John nodded slowly and then said,

"You could work on that you know."

"It's probably a little late to take up jogging, don't you think?"

There was a touch in fatalism in Robert's voice which John had never heard before. He also was not making eye contact; instead he was looking out the window.

"How worried are you? Is there anything I can do? Do you want me there?" Then John asked,

"Have you told your kids?"

Robert didn't talk to his two sons, one of whom lived in China where he worked managing a manufacturing plant for an American shoe company. It would not have surprised John to know Robert hadn't talked to either one in over a year. He didn't know exactly happened between them, but knew that when their mother died his sons didn't seem to have much use for their dad.

"I'm sure you have better things to do than sit around a hospital waiting for me to wake up after surgery. What about that kid you interviewed? What's the story on him? How did your board meeting go?"

John decided two things right then. If Robert didn't want to talk about his kids that was his choice. John asked them for their contact information when he did their mother's funeral and would let them know what was happening with their father. He would also be sure to be at the hospital when Robert had his surgery.

"I suspect I'm going to hire him. The board meeting didn't exactly go as we planned; in fact, we didn't get around to talking about Edward."

"What do you mean it didn't go as you planned?"

John had not talked with Robert about what had been consuming him for the past few weeks. He was reluctant to go over it all again with someone else and let Robert's question hang in the air while he thought.

"I have a member of my church whose husband is dying of a brain tumor. She's come to me asking why God won't heal her husband. She's trying to understand why it seems to say in the Bible God will answer our prayers. She asked me if I have ever prayed for someone to be healed and they were. I had to say no. We talked about this at our meeting." John waited for a moment and then asked Robert,

"Have you?"

Robert was usually not at a loss for words, but he was silent as he thought back over his long career as a pastor. When he finally spoke John was surprised at his words.

"I usually didn't pray for people to be healed. Sometimes, but most of the time I prayed they would find comfort in their suffering. So to answer your question, no, I have never prayed for someone who was in a situation like you're describing and they were healed."

"You didn't pray for people to be healed? Why not? Is there a reason?"

"John, I seldom thought I knew what God wanted for the people in my churches in terms of the specific things in their life, including their health. I always knew, however, God wanted them to find comfort in their suffering and to learn to trust Him in difficult circumstances. Maybe it's because I don't have a lot of faith, I don't know. Maybe I found it easier to pray for the spiritual needs of people rather than their physical needs because then I wouldn't have to look for a physical result. I will say, though, nobody ever came to me with the question of why God won't heal my husband. What did you tell her?"

"I told her I have prayed that God would heal her husband."

It was clear to Robert, as it had been to John's board, what John meant by those words. Robert sipped his coffee and thought about the implication of what John was saying. Before he could respond, the waitress came and took their order, giving Robert a few more moments to think about what John had said.

"And what did she take away from that?"

"I'm not sure, but I don't think I helped her much. She's exhausted by everything she's been going through."

"So she doesn't believe her husband is going to be healed?" Robert did not ask this as a question, he said it as a realization of what he thought Robin took from what John had told her.

"I suspect that she doesn't believe her husband is going to be healed."

"And you're okay leaving her like that?"

"Robert, I don't know what I'm okay with. I just know that Jesus said that if we ask him for something he will do it. I would like to see him do something big once in my life."

"You don't consider God answering what we might call regular prayers "something big"?

"I think you know what I mean."

"Yeah, I do know what you mean, that's the problem. You're in a tough spot personally and you think that if God does a miracle it will jumpstart your faith. You may not have had this thought, but I can assure you that it's there just below the surface. And you didn't answer my question, are you okay leaving her like that? That you believe her husband is going to be healed?"

John had assured Amy his prayer for Jerry to be healed had nothing to do with him, but now he was not so sure. All he wanted to do was take God at his word and have him do something for someone else. He didn't want to make it more than that, but he knew people seldom did things with completely pure motives. He didn't want to add to Robin's burden, he just wanted her to know...what?

Their food arrived while John was having these thoughts, though he had lost his appetite. He didn't know how to answer Robert. On one level he wanted Robin to know there was still hope for her husband and that he believed God was bigger than Jerry's tumor. Yet, for the first time since he sat in the chapel and prayed for Jerry, he was not sure. He thought of the man who asked Jesus to heal his son, who believed Jesus could do that but also realized his faith was still incomplete. John felt the same way; he knew Jesus could heal Jerry but he did not want to have any doubts. He wondered if that was possible.

Robert interrupted his train of thought when he slowly repeated, "Are you okay leaving her like that?"

Robert was surprised by what John said next.

"Why are you assuming that God is not going heal her husband?"

Neither one of them had touched their food; it sat in front of them as they talked. They had never had a conversation quite like this before, one that was complex and touched on so many different areas of life. One that literally dealt with life and death. Most of the time they talked about what was going on in John's church, which was enough to keep them going for their time together each week.

Robert did not want to admit he was assuming God would not heal the man, but he knew what John was saying was probably true. Like John, Robert had never seen anyone with cancer healed, so it seemed reasonable to think this situation would be like all of the others he witnessed over the years. People get cancer; some beat it, some die. None get healed. Robert believed God could heal anyone of anything, but he also knew people die every day; the young, the old, children, brothers, sisters, wives and husbands. Why would God single out one man to heal and let everyone else die?

He knew Jesus himself acted in that manner. He healed some, he didn't heal all. To heal one lame man he stepped over many others who were suffering, some perhaps more. It dawned on Robert it wasn't the fact that God might heal the man that was difficult to accept, it was the fact that John seemed to know God was going to heal him that was troubling.

"How do you know God is going to heal this man? Did he tell you?"

"Robert, I have prayed God would heal Jerry and that he would become a Christian."

"But you believe this is going to happen, that he's going to be healed?"

"You sound just like my board. They're more concerned about what the aftermath will be if Jerry isn't healed. They don't want to accept the possibility God will do something big, because they're afraid if he doesn't they won't know how to react."

"I'm just like your board. I'm a man of little faith and many doubts. I don't doubt God can do anything he wants, it's just when I don't see him healing terminally ill people all the time I figure there must be a reason."

"So what's the reason?"

"John, I just don't know."

John didn't know either, and though his conversation caused him to doubt, he could live with that. He suspected he wasn't the first person who believed God was going to do a miracle and then had second thoughts. He thought back to the conversation he had with Robin when she asked him if he ever prayed for someone who had then been healed. When he said no, he remembered her words that maybe this would be the first time. There was nowhere else for the conversation to go, so John said,

"Let's eat before our food gets cold."

14

John spent the rest of the afternoon in his office. He planned on using the time to work on his message, but his mind was not free from the discussion he had with Robert that morning. On the drive to his office he had time to think about what Robert had said, primarily about how he was a man of little faith and many doubts. John knew everyone had moments of clarity regarding their faith and moments when faith rolled out with the tide. He didn't know how to define what great faith was and what it might look like in different situations. He didn't know where the line between faith and presumption was, the last thing he wanted to do was to presume he knew what God wanted. What was wrong with presumption, though, if you based it on what God said in the Bible?

Certainly you could presume that God loved you. Certainly you could presume that he wanted the best for you. Certainly you could presume that God would do what he said. John was not naïve enough to believe that because God loved everyone and healed people throughout the Bible he could presume that God would heal everyone. He had met people who believed that you could presume God would heal everyone and if he didn't the problem was not God's but a lack of faith on the part of the person asking to be healed. Jesus talked about having faith as a condition of being healed, but then there were times when he healed those who were not given the opportunity to exhibit any faith at all.

John thought about the fairness of only answering the prayers of those who had great faith. If God only answered the prayers of those who already believed he would answer, wasn't he treating his children differently? How were the weak in faith supposed to develop faith if in their weakness they never saw God answer any of their prayers?

His notebook containing his prayer requests was lying on one side of his desk. If you looked at it from one point of view, it was a book filled with answers that mostly fell into the realm of "no" and "not yet". If you looked at it from another point of view it was a book that screamed to him "Why won't you believe, so I can answer your prayers?" On the other side of his desk was his Bible. If you looked at it from one point of view it was a book that said "Ask and you shall receive", with no conditions whatsoever. If you looked at it from another point of view it said, "Ask according to God's will and he hears us." How could John ask God what his will for Jerry was? If he did, then what was the use praying for something that he already knew was going to happen?

John thought about what Robert said regarding his faith needing to be jumpstarted. That he might be looking for a miracle as much for himself as for Jerry and Robin. He didn't think that was true, but he was in a tough spot personally. He had prayed for a child for six years and finally knew that the answer was "no". He could live with that. He could even live with Sharon's refusal to consider adoption. But he was wondering if he could live with a God who would not come out into the open and do something big, something mighty, something miraculous.

He was interrupted in his thought when Susan knocked lightly on his door and then opened it to speak to him. He motioned her in and asked her to sit in the chair in front of his desk. He asked her what she needed.

"You asked me to set up a meeting with Edward. He's available any evening you would like to meet with him." She paused briefly, and then said,

"Are you going to hire him?"

She was always fishing, John thought, but not necessarily in a bad way. Her world revolved around the church and adding another staff member would change the dynamic in her workplace.

John always appreciated that Susan was generally up front with him. He never had to worry about what she was thinking, what she felt about someone or her opinion if asked. He felt bad about what he was going to ask her, but he felt she probably represented a point of view that was common in the church.

"Can I ask you a question?"

"Of course. You can ask me anything you want."

John often used Susan as a sounding board for different ideas that ran through his head regarding sermons, people, church operations and other matters, though he seldom asked her opinion about anything related to his personal life.

"When was the last time you knew God answered one of your prayers?"

She was caught completely off guard and somewhat speechless. After a moment she said,

"What do you mean?"

"I think the question speaks for itself."

"I pray all the time. You know that."

"I know. I'm just asking you to tell me a prayer God has answered recently in your life."

She was searching her mind trying to think of something she could say in response. With a sense of relief she said to John,

"I prayed that Sarah Mickelson would get the job she was applying for. She started work yesterday."

John thought a moment before he responded.

"I prayed for Sarah, too. How do you know God answered that prayer and Sarah just wasn't the best person that company looked at? People get hired everyday who have never prayed for a job."

"Are you saying God didn't answer my prayer?"

"I don't know. I just know there is another explanation for Sarah getting that job. What I'm asking you is if you have had a prayer answered where there is no other explanation than God did something for you."

When she didn't answer after a few moments, John said,

"I don't mean to make you uncomfortable, but this is what I have been dealing with the last several weeks."

"Are you headed for a fall? About all of this with Jerry?"

He still could not get over the fact that no one seemed to believe God would heal Jerry. Everyone assumed he was going to die and John would then fall apart and the fallout would somehow affect the church. Then it hit him. The board was thinking about what would happen to the church if it became known John believed Jerry was going to be healed, and then he died. The board liked it when things were normal and John had taken them way past normal.

"Susan, I believe God is bigger than any fall that could happen to me. I'll be alright."

"I hope so. I'd hate to lose you."

Where did that come from, he thought. He looked at her with a puzzled expression and she realized instantly she had gone too far. Michael had shared with her his thought that if Jerry died John might not be able to handle the disappointment and leave the church. Michael was reading more into John's words than he should, but Susan did not know that.

"Why don't you call Edward back and have him come by Thursday around 7. If everything goes as planned I'll probably hire him. What do you think?"

Susan was thinking she was glad the subject was changed and she could leave.

"I think he would be a good addition to our church."

With that she was up and gone from his office, closing the door softly behind her. John wondered if she would think about the question he had asked her about God answering her prayers. Probably not right then, but maybe the next time she prayed. He did not mean to cause anyone to doubt, but he also thought it wasn't fair that he seemed to be the only one who was grappling with this issue. He wasn't, as he would find out shortly.

15

The board did not usually meet more than once a month, but John wanted to introduce Edward to them and get him before the church as soon as possible. Edward spent a day with John earlier that week. They talked about how Edward would approach the job. What he thought he would need to be successful. A time table of when he would recruit leaders, train them and then promote and launch small groups. John had come to realize that Edward had more depth than his age and experience at first suggested. He did not tell Edward anything about the members of the board, or what to expect, so that he would be as spontaneous as possible.

They spent a few minutes chatting among themselves before John asked Tim to open the meeting with prayer. Edward seemed to be at ease among the older men and had no trouble joining in the conversation before the meeting. In his prayer Tim specifically prayed for Robin and Jerry, and as John listened he sensed the meeting might not go as he planned.

It was Wayne, who asked him,

"How are they doing?"

John had talked to Edward about Jerry and he guessed Edward made the connection to their earlier conversation about unanswered prayer.

"I talked with Robin yesterday. She's about the same. Jerry is worse. The doctors don't think that he has very long."

There was a period of silence that did not surprise John as the group waited for someone to speak. John suspected it would be Tim who would want to stay on the subject, and he was right.

"How are you feeling about this? Did you tell Robin what you told us about Jerry being healed?"

"I told Robin the same thing I said here, that I have prayed for Jerry to be healed. I know you have also prayed for him to be healed. Robin has also prayed for Jerry to be healed."

"But John", Tim continued, "It seemed to us that you fully expect Jerry to be healed. Isn't that right?"

John wasn't afraid to say what he believed, but he also wanted to help the group think through some of the issues he was dealing with. He refused to answer the question the way Tim wanted.

"Tim, I believe that God answers our prayers. I believe he knows what is best for us. I believe he will answer this prayer. Don't you?"

"Yes, I do. But maybe not in the same way that you expect."

"I haven't told you what I expect, only that I have prayed for Jerry to be healed, as have you."

Tim was obviously frustrated but saw no point in continuing the conversation. Michael, however, wasn't quite ready to move on to talking about Edward. Edward was sitting quietly in his chair, certainly not expecting the type of meeting unfolding before him.

"Did you imply to Robin that Jerry is going to be healed? John, how is she going to feel if he dies? How will you explain that to her?"

"I think a lot of this is premature. Despite how some of you are talking, Jerry is not dead yet. I think Robin is under a lot of stress right now, and I know she hasn't been getting much sleep. Let's think about how we can support her and wait and see how God is going to work."

John's tone suggested he wanted to move the conversation along and had it been a normal meeting the board would have followed his lead. But this was not a normal meeting and not everyone had a chance to weigh in. Now it was Wayne's turn.

"John, we all want to support Robin in any way we can. But I think you can understand our concern about giving her hope that Jerry will be healed. I know we all believe that God can do that if he wants, but it seems in this case, for whatever the reason, he's not going to heal Jerry."

"If you'll pardon how I phrase this, let me play devil's advocate for a moment. Wayne, what makes you think it's not God's will to heal Jerry?"

"You mean beside the fact he's almost dead?"

"Yes, beside the fact that he's almost dead." John waited for Wayne to answer.

"Well, I suppose that if he was going to be healed God would have done it by now."

"So when God heals people he does it before they get really sick and near death?"

"I didn't mean it that way. I guess I'm just not accustomed to God healing people with brain tumors who are near death. I've never heard of anything like that before. You're the one who said you'd never prayed for anyone like Jerry who has healed. I guess I want to know what makes you think this time will be different."

"I never said this time would be different. I've only said I have prayed that God would heal Jerry and open his heart to believe. What I am learning is we cannot put God in a box made up of how we think he's going to work."

It was all too much for Michael. He was listening to John talk and was tired of what he perceived as his evasiveness.

"John, why won't you tell us if you believe Jerry is going to be healed? Am I the only one who thinks you're talking in circles?"

John knew Michael was not the only one having that thought. He was not trying to create confusion or doubt. He also didn't think it was a bad thing for them to continue to discuss why and how God works in people's lives.

"If I told you I knew Jerry was going to be healed, would that make you believe? Would that increase your faith? Make you more obedient or love God more? I doubt it. I think you want to know for the same reason Peter asked Jesus what was going to happen to John. We want to know about what God is going to do with other people rather than letting him work in our own lives. I'm not saying this is how you think, but I know this is how I think much of the time. I also believe we're looking for what we think is going to happen, instead of waiting to see what God is going to do."

Instead of responding to John, Michael turned to Edward and said,

"I would like to bring Edward into the conversation. I know that he doesn't know the whole situation, but since he's here I wonder what he thinks about why God does or doesn't heal people when we pray for them."

John could have intervened and let Edward off the hook he was about to be hung on, but he didn't. He wanted to know what Edward was thinking about the conversation he had been listening to and how he would respond to the men he would be working for.

Edward, however, did not mind joining the conversation. Unlike the rest of the men in the room, Edward had seen God heal someone with a terminal disease, someone who was given no chance to live. It happened on a mission trip he took while in college, and though the person was healed, it did not turn out well. Though the board may have thought it might have been relevant to the conversation, he decided not to bring it up.

"I believe it's never wrong to pray for the things we want. I don't always know what God's will is, but I know that it's never wrong to ask. I think sometimes we ask God to do things for reasons we may not completely understand, and get disappointed when God doesn't answer in the way we want."

Edward wasn't thinking about John when he spoke, but Wayne was. Wayne knew John had been faithfully praying for some people for years. He always regarded that as an indication that John was a man of faith. Someone who did not give up on God despite many of those prayers not being answered. Now Wayne was wondering if John was forcing the issue with Jerry to put God to the test. When no one immediately responded, Edward continued.

"When I pray for people, I use the prayers of Paul as a guide. He prayed for people to be strong in their faith, to love Jesus more, to know the will of God, to be obedient and to be wise in how they talk to people. I don't often see Paul praying for physical needs; it was the spiritual needs of people that concerned him."

He realized as the words left him it could be interpreted he was contradicting everything John was saying. The board was certain that John was saying Jerry was going to be healed, and now Edward was saying Paul never prayed for people to be healed. He quickly added,

"But I guess Paul did pray for himself to be healed when he had his thorn in the flesh. So maybe there's another side to all of this. It's hard to be really dogmatic when you're talking about something that has many sides to it."

"It seems to me", Michael said, "That God didn't answer Paul's prayer to be healed, did he?"

Wayne wanted to change the direction of the conversation and talk with Edward about the position he was applying for. Wayne thought they had taken this about as far as they could. He did not want the board to become consumed by Jerry's situation as he thought it was consuming John. He said,

"I think we all realize God sometimes doesn't answer our prayers the way we want. But like Paul, we come to realize that he knows best. And we should trust him however he answers."

John knew what Wayne was trying to do, but was not quite ready to let it go. He didn't mind Edward offering a different perspective because he knew something Edward did not, and he knew Edward was not trying to provoke him or make points with the board. His last words on the subject were,

"You're right Wayne; God didn't answer Paul's prayer the way he wanted. But Paul knew when the prayer was answered, didn't he?

God told him after the third request he was going to have to live with his thorn. Can any of us say that God has answered our prayer, either yes or no, about Jerry as of today?"

When no one responded, John said,

"Then let's wait and see what he's going to do."

They spent the next two hours talking with Edward about his life, education, previous experience and how he would fit into their church. John let the board do most of the talking. His mind was somewhere else. The one recurring thought he kept having was that at their next board meeting he knew exactly what they were going to talk about.

16

Thursday 7.00 pm

John found time the next afternoon to begin shaping the message he wanted to give on Sunday. He did not interact much with Susan during the day. She left without saying goodbye, something she had never done before. From his window, he saw her walk to her car at precisely 5 p.m., get in and drive away without looking back. John had not meant to offend her or cause her any type of discomfort. Susan was generally not an introspective person, so he doubted she spent much time after their conversation thinking about what he said to her. Or maybe she had, which could account for her behavior.

John had thought about little else for most of the last two weeks. His mind kept going to the same place over and over again: a knot he could not untie. Every conversation he had with different people left him back at the beginning. He found in books and different places on the Internet those who had proposed answers for the questions he was asking. He generally found they gave him little help.

Those who tried to explain why God answered some prayers and not others (though they used the same reasoning as John when he told people that "no" is still an answer) usually followed the same line of reasoning. John thought it interesting that no one seriously addressed the question haunting him, Why won't God answer my prayer the way I want when it seems to say (especially from Jesus' own words) that he will? People took stabs at the answer, but John found most of them unsatisfying.

Nearly everyone said you had to pray with the right motives or God would not answer your prayers. In the case of Jerry, John was convinced that his only motive was for Jerry to be healed and become a Christian. He knew his own heart and did not think there was anything in this for him if God healed Jerry. In this he would find out he was wrong.

Others who wrote on the subject stressed that you needed to pray in the will of God, but John did not know what God's will for Jerry was. If he knew God's will for Jerry, why would he need to pray?

He found most commentators and bloggers also brought out the idea that if you had sin in your heart God would not answer your prayers. John agreed, but had the thought everyone has sin in their heart. It must be the seriousness and degree that concerned God. John wasn't perfect, but he didn't think this was a reason God would not answer his prayer.

Some brought up the issue of timing. God would answer when the time was right and not before. This did not pertain to Jerry because his time was running out. In fact; John was surprised he was still alive.

Robert said he was a man of little faith and many doubts. This reason was brought up by some as why God would not answer prayer. John's dilemma was he sincerely believed God could do anything and basically told his board and Robin he believed God was going to heal Jerry. John did not know how to measure faith, and he did not know when faith turned into presumption.

There was one writer who suggested from a verse in John 15 that if you weren't reading the Bible, God would not answer your prayers. John read the Bible every day, which caused him to think that he was perhaps reading it too much and had developed a rut that was displeasing to God. He dismissed the thought out of hand when it occurred to him he was probably way overthinking the issue.

Finally, there was one reason he could not get past. Everyone said the same thing about God; that he knew best and would answer prayers in a manner that was the best for everyone involved. But John could not get past the fact that the best thing for Jerry, Robin and their kids was for Jerry be healed and become a Christian. He knew God could bring good out of every kind of tragedy and suffering, but he always came back to the same place. Why does God so seldom answer prayers that would be considered miraculous?

John understood the danger that some brought up: if God answered prayers that involved healing, dramatic deliverance from unfavorable circumstances or anything involving the miraculous, that would be all Christians would pray for. Prayers for endurance, prayers for character, prayers for faith, prayers for understanding; these types of prayers would be forgotten if God did the big, miraculous things people wanted for their lives.

If it weren't for the seemingly unconditional promises that God would answer prayer, John could live with the reasons he found why God wouldn't answer prayer. John also wondered if God wanted his children obsessing about those reasons in regards to how they approached him. Do I have sin in my heart? Is this the will of God? Do I have enough faith? Am I spending enough time in the Bible? Am I praying about this enough? It seemed to him you could spend your life trying to be good enough for God to answer your prayers. John was sure that was not the way God wanted his children to think of him.

John stayed at church instead of going home in anticipation of his meeting with Edward. He called Sharon and left a message on her cell phone saying he would not be home for dinner. They were at an impasse but he didn't care. He did not have enough energy to deal with trying to find out what was going on in her mind. His talk with Amy and her father gave him some insight into her that he suspected, but not known for sure. That insight meant he could be more direct the next time they spoke about their future, a prospect he did not relish.

Edward arrived at the church just before seven. John met him at the door and brought him to his office. They chatted for a moment about the unusually nice weather that spring and about Edward's interest in the local baseball team. John, though he followed sports, did not have the devotion that characterized a fan. After a time John began by asking Edward what he thought about the board meeting.

"It wasn't what I expected. What did you think about it?"

This was the second time Edward turned a question back to him. John was beginning to understand that Edward had more depth and experience than he initially thought.

"I assume you're talking about the man who is ill. This wasn't the first time it had been discussed. We usually talk about issues that aren't so complex or theological. I think the board is waiting to see what's going to happen, and then I suspect we'll talk some more. I wasn't just playing devil's advocate, trying to get them to think with me about our relationship to God and how he works in our lives."

"Do you think you succeeded?"

"I thought I was the one who was supposed to ask the questions."

John smiled when he spoke. He wasn't put off by Edward asking him questions, but it caused him to think what their working relationship would be like. He was used to being in charge at the church; even the board didn't ask lots of questions. Except for the last two meetings.

"Sorry. Asking questions just comes naturally to me. It helps when you're working with kids. It lets them know you're interested."

John said in response,

"I've learned that most of the time you can't change the way people think or behave by giving them facts, principles or even the truth. You have to put it before them and let them decide what they want to do with it. When I learned this, after years of trying to fix people or get them to agree with me, it was quite refreshing. It took a burden off me that I willingly gave to God. I'll lead them to the water, he can make them drink." He paused, then continued,

"When people come to me with their problems and difficulties, I ask them lots of questions, too. If they can arrive at the same solution I would give them, they might actually follow through and find the relief or comfort they desire."

Edward nodded in agreement, and then John realized Edward had not answered his question about the board meeting. John said,

"You haven't answered my question about the board meeting."

"No, I haven't."

John waited as Edward thought how to respond. The board meeting brought back memories for Edward that he had not thought about for many years. Memories that were not pleasant. He could just let it slide, or he could bring them up with John. It was directly related to what was happening in John's life, but Edward realized it could complicate things for him.

"When I was in college I went on a mission trip to southern Mexico. There were ten of us and we went to work with a small church that had a connection to one of the pastors at our church. We went down to do evangelism with the local kids. We brought soccer balls, nets, uniforms, shoes, things that were not available to them. Things they could never have afforded.

"After one game, we were asked to visit the home of one particular kid. It was just a shack really. Couple of rooms, cooking out back. The dad was in one of the rooms, lying on a mat. He was obviously sick, though we didn't know how badly until our interpreter started asking questions. It turned out he was dying, or so they said. The one doctor in the town said there wasn't anything he could do for the man and said they better call the priest. We asked what was wrong with him, but no one really knew. They asked us to pray for him, which we did. I remember we all prayed the man would be healed. Whether we believed it or not, I don't know to this day. We were asked to pray, so we did.

"The next day we were playing soccer at the town field, right around noon. The kid whose dad was ill comes running across the field and starts grabbing at us, talking a mile a minute. None of us spoke Spanish, so someone went and found our interpreter and brought him back to the field. The kid told the interpreter his dad wasn't sick anymore and we should go see him. Well, we were completely surprised, to say the least. I remember thinking he probably was feeling better because we prayed for him, not that he was healed."

Edward stopped talking and spent a moment remembering. He continued by saying,

"I'm here to tell you he was completely better. The doctor was there that morning and said he could find nothing wrong with the man. When we saw him he was at the back of his house cooking tortillas with his wife over an open fire, looking like he didn't have a care in the world. When he saw us coming he ran to us and started kissing our hands and thanking us over and over. By later in the afternoon word had gotten around the village and people were coming to his little shack to see for themselves. I learned a new Spanish word that day. Milagro. You can guess what it means."

Edward got up from the chair and looked out the office window at the parking lot. He was now talking to himself; it was as if John was not in the room.

"That night at dinner we were still excited about the whole thing. None of us had ever seen anything like that before. And then someone said, I wonder if he was really that sick. That sucked all the air out of the room. I mean it was like turning off a light and being plunged into total darkness. That question divided us into two groups, one that believed the man had been healed and another that didn't deny it, but had questions or other explanations. Questions like, I've heard of cases where people seemed to be healed but after a while they just get worse. Or, Maybe the doctor totally misdiagnosed him. Or, What if he gets sick again, will they be mad at us? Or, Let's see how he is in the morning, with the implication that his healing might not stand the night.

"At any rate, our euphoria lasted part of an afternoon, and then it was gone. The real problems began the next morning. We were sleeping at the little church and as soon as it was light the people of the village started bringing people to us. We were just college students, so what did we know about healing people? However, we spent the morning praying for everyone they brought to us. The man we had prayed for first came too. He was still looking completely well, which gave us some confidence in praying for everyone else."

He turned away from the window and sat back down.

"That was the end of our trip. We couldn't go anywhere in the town without people coming to us with their sick friends and family. People who probably were just going to get better in the normal course of life, and some who were really sick. We had to leave the next day because the word had spread to other villages and our leader thought it was going to get out of control. Which is kind of funny when you think about it."

"Did anyone else get healed that you know of?"

"I don't think so. The interpreter we used went back months later to find out what happened to the man who has healed. It turned out he was fine and had started going to the village church with his family. I guess he was kind of like a celebrity."

"What do you think happened?"

"I think God healed the man. Why him and apparently no one else, I can't tell you. But it cut our trip short and we didn't go home as elated as you might think. In fact, the leader of our group actually cautioned us against telling people the man had been healed because we didn't actually know for a fact that was what happened."

"What do you think he was afraid of?"

"It was a she, the head of the English department. You have to remember, we went to a conservative Christian college. Healing people was for other denominations and groups; it didn't fit into our theology and practice. I think she meant well, but looking back you're right. She was more than a little fearful of what might happen if we told people we prayed for a man who was dying and he got better."

They saw the irony in the situation that was John was in. Except for one glaring difference. Jerry was still dying, and there was no miracle.

"I'm glad you didn't share this story with the board. It would just serve to complicate things. Thanks."

"I thought about it. But that wasn't why you brought me to the meeting, was it?"

"No, it wasn't."

John had some misgivings he would not be able to explain to the board, but then he knew he would never find a perfect person to bring into the church.

"When can you start?"

17

He was surprised Sharon was still awake when he returned home later that evening. She was usually in bed by 9 so she could rise early and spend time reading the Bible. John knew there was something bothering her when he came into the kitchen. She was sitting at the table with her arms crossed. He went to the refrigerator to get a glass of water and waited for her to speak.

"Why did you go talk to my father?"

John leaned back against the sink and took a long drink, suddenly feeling very tired. It had been a long day, and he did not think he had the strength to have a conversation that promised to be emotionally draining. He also wondered how she found out about his meeting with Mr. Banks. It was an easy way to begin.

"How did you find out about that?"

"I called my mother to see how she's feeling. She said that you met with him this week. Why would you do that?"

"How is your mom doing? Is she any better?"

"That's really not the point. He came home upset and he won't tell her why. Just that he met with you for breakfast."

John was surprised that Mrs. Banks would have the nerve to ask her husband why he might be upset about something. He was also surprised by the fact that Mr. Banks did not get his emotions under control by the time he returned home.

"Why won't either of you tell me how your mother is feeling? I know that she hasn't been doing well for some time. Is it something serious?"

"My father can look after her. She's well enough to call and tell me that he was upset with you."

There were two directions he could take the conversation, and he was tempted to take the easy way out. He knew Mr. Banks would never tell either Sharon or his wife what they talked about. John could make something up and get out relatively unscathed. He wouldn't exactly lie, but he didn't have to reveal everything about their conversation. On one level John wanted to spare her the questions he needed to ask. On another level he wanted to get answers to questions he knew had shaped Sharon's life and were influencing their future together. He took the plunge.

"I went to talk with him about you. Your upbringing, what you were like as a kid, what he was like as a father. Plus, I haven't seen him in ages and thought it would be good to get together."

It wasn't exactly a lie, but Sharon knew John and her father had virtually no relationship and there wasn't much point in trying to begin one after so many years.

"Besides the fact I doubt he would tell you anything, why would you need to know about how I was raised?"

"You're wrong about that, he was actually very open. I was pleasantly surprised."

She laughed at the thought of her father sharing anything about his children and how they were raised. Sharon didn't laugh because the thought struck her as funny; she laughed knowing it could not be true.

"My father talking about how he raised my brother and me? You have got to be kidding. He would never do that. Never in a million years."

It occurred to John he'd never heard Sharon use any other term than "father" to refer to Mr. Banks, though she did refer to her mother as "mom".

"Do you want me to tell you what he told me?"

Now Sharon wasn't laughing. She looked at John suspiciously, with her eyes narrowed.

"No, I don't."

"Well, I think you should hear it. He said you were an obedient child who always did what he asked. That you did those things because it was what he expected of you. And you knew what the consequences would be if you didn't obey. Does that sound about right?"

She was the least introspective person John had ever met, though this did not become clear to him until a few years into their marriage. Sharon never talked about the past, didn't dwell on the future, and outwardly maintained a tight control on her emotions. He came to see that her defining character trait was to do what she believed was right. He was now coming to see that her motivation for doing what was right might be different from what he believed in the past. When she didn't answer he said,

"I also asked him if you were a happy kid growing up. He basically told me he considers happiness to be sinful. You don't think that do you?"

"My father told us being obedient to God was what mattered. Not some ill-defined concept of happiness. And yes, I believe that if you're looking to be happy all the time you will seldom be obedient."

"You don't think God wants us to be happy? To enjoy life?"

"I didn't say that. If you have to talk about being happy, then I would say the more you obey God the happier you'll be. I don't know why you're bringing this up. I've always tried to do what you wanted, to make you happy if you want to put it that way."

It was true. Sharon had always tried to do what she thought would make John happy, though she would not have put it that way. He was seeing her now in a completely different light than he had in the past. If what he was thinking was true it was not pretty.

"Just like you tried to make your dad happy by obeying him as best you could?"

She could not answer his question, though the answer was obvious on her face. She had spent her whole life trying to make two men happy. One destroyed her by communicating in different ways she could never meet his expectations and the other who never realized what she was trying to do until now. He didn't know how to end the conversation, but he found it would end with her saying, as she rose from the table,

"I told you, I'm not something you need to fix. And don't talk to my father again."

She turned and went down the hallway toward the bedroom, leaving him standing against the kitchen counter. He would give her some time, and then follow her. It might take her a day or two to get past this conversation, but he knew that she would. To let it linger would be a sign of weakness. He was glad he opened the door, but he didn't know where it was going to lead.

In his dealings with people over the years, when doors to the past were opened they either went through and dealt with what they found or stopped coming to see him. Sharon wasn't somebody he was counseling, but he wondered if the pattern would be the same. She wouldn't leave him, but she might close up tight if he continued down memory lane with her. He rubbed his eyes and thought what a long day it had been. Just as he set his glass down and was ready to go to bed, his cell phone went off in his shirt pocket. Hoping it was not something that would result in him having to go out into the night; he looked at the screen and took in a quick breath. It was Robin.

Part Two

1

Thursday 11.00 pm

It occurred to him after he left the house and was almost to the hospital he had not told Sharon he was leaving. She undoubtedly heard him shut the front door and start his car; in light of their conversation he had no idea what she might be thinking. The sudden surge of adrenalin he got after he spoke to Robin cleared his mind and gave him the energy he needed for what he was going to face.

John knew this day was coming; cancer had a way of forcing the inevitable. Their conversation was short and one sided. She asked him to come to the hospital right away and when he said yes, she hung up. Despite the adrenalin, he was calm and not worrying about what he was going to say to Robin when he arrived. This would change everything for the foreseeable future, not only for him but for any number of other people. The thought that kept going through his mind was to be there for Robin, everything else would sort itself out in the coming days.

Hospitals at night have an atmosphere all their own. Though there were people coming and going, there was little talk and the lighting was much dimmer. If you are at the hospital late at night and not working, it is usually because something bad has happened. John walked through the front doors and toward the elevators that lead to Jerry's room. He rode the elevator alone and prayed that he would be equal to the task ahead of him.

He came out of the elevator and turned to the right to make his way to the ICU. There was no one else on the floor, which puzzled him. He came to the ICU door and rang the intercom so a nurse could open the metal door and let him in. After waiting for a more than a moment, he pushed the button again. Finally, he could hear someone walking toward the door, and then it opened out toward him. A nurse looked him over and said,

"You're the pastor?"

"Yeah. Robin called me and asked me to come."

The nurse would not take her eyes off him, and he suddenly felt embarrassed standing in front of her. He broke the spell by saying,

"Can I come in?"

In what seemed to John totally inappropriate, she smiled and said,

"You sure can."

She grabbed him by the arm, and still smiling led him past the nurse's station toward Jerry's room. When they turned a corner of the hallway he could see Jerry's room. He was startled to see a group of nurses standing outside the door looking in. The nurse guiding him still gripped his arm and gently pushed the nurses aside so they could get in the room. This is what he saw.

Robin was standing on one side of the bed holding Jerry's hand. Where there had been IV's, tubes and lines running into Jerry, there was now nothing. Even the monitors that measured Jerry's vital signs were gone. Jerry himself was sitting upright, eating a meal that was on a tray placed over his lap. John didn't understand.

When Robin saw him standing in the door trying to comprehend what was going on, she came around the side of the bed and without a word wrapped her arms around him tightly, not letting go for what seemed like forever. The nurses who were watching were all smiles, enjoying something they seldom, if ever, experienced. When Robin let go she said to John,

"Let's talk outside."

As he left the room he took another look at Jerry, still peacefully eating his meal, apparently without a care in the world. Robin led him back out the ICU doors to the waiting area. They sat down on chairs opposite each other and John waited for Robin to speak. But she just looked down at her hands and could not stop smiling. John broke the silence and asked,

"What's going on?"

Robin looked up and with tears falling down her cheeks, said,

"What do you think is going on? Jerry's been healed. You believed it would happen and it did. I don't know how to thank you."

It made sense to him, having witnessed what was happening in Jerry's room, but John did not know how to respond. His mind was in one place, wanting to find a way to begin asking questions of Robin. His emotions were somewhere else, slowly starting to catch up to reality. When he finally spoke he simply said,

"Tell me what's happened."

Robin slowly began to detail for him the events of the day which had brought them to this moment.

"I came in this morning to see Jerry and he was the same. Unresponsive and in and out of consciousness. I left before lunch to run some errands and then I got a call around 1 from his doctor. He said I needed to get back to the hospital. When I asked why he just said that I needed to come back. I knew this was coming, but I don't think you can ever prepare yourself for something like that."

She paused as she thought about what transpired just hours before.

"When I got to his room there were nurses standing just outside the door, like they're doing now. It didn't seem right, they were talking and some were even laughing. I've been here when people have died and that is not how the nurses act. The doctor was beside his bed, taking the IV lines out of his arm. Jerry was sitting up in bed looking perfectly normal, telling the doctor how he felt. Jerry hadn't spoken in days so I just stood there and didn't know what to say.

"The doctor took me outside the room and told me Jerry woke up just after I left and asked if he could have something to eat. He told the nurses he was feeling fine, so they called the doctor to have him examine Jerry. Jerry told the doctor he felt great and asked if he could see me. I guess it happens that sometimes cancer patients have this moment of clarity before they die, but the doctor had never seen anything like this before. After about an hour they took him down to x ray. It's gone, John. The tumor is gone. The doctor can't explain it, but he can't deny it either. You saw that all of his tubes and stuff are gone. It's been almost 12 hours. It's all anyone on the floor is talking about."

He had an uneasy sense of foreboding, that events were going to take on a life of their own and he was going to be an observer like everyone else. He asked a question when he felt he already knew the answer.

"What are they saying"?

"They know it's a miracle. I told them my pastor prayed for Jerry to be healed. That's the only explanation. They believe it because they've never seen anything like this before. They all knew Jerry wasn't going to go home. That he was going to die here."

Robin was looking at John, puzzled by his response to what was happening in her life.

"Is everything alright? I thought you'd be happy. You were the only one to believe this was going to happen."

The last thing he wanted at that moment was to talk about what he believed was or was not going to happen.

"I am so happy for you. It's been a long day and I guess my emotions are lagging behind what's going on. When are they going to let Jerry go home?"

"I don't think the doctor quite believes what's happened, so he wants Jerry to stay another day and then do one final x ray. Then he says if everything is clear he can go home."

"Have you told the girls?"

"Tomorrow morning I'm going to bring them to see their dad. I want it to be special so I'm not going to tell them before they see him."

"You should go home and get some sleep. I think the next few days are going to be long. Good, but long." John paused for a moment, wanting to ask her one more question. The adrenalin rush had passed, and he was feeling the effects of the long day. He wanted to ask the question in the right manner, but in his fatigue it came out sounding wrong.

"Did you tell anyone else?"

Robin heard the hesitation in John's voice and misunderstood, she thought he was just tired.

"Not yet, but I plan to. It's not every day you get a miracle. I want everyone to know what you did for my family."

He was tired, but not too tired to know he shouldn't say anything that would spoil this moment for Robin. God was there for her when she thought he wasn't, and who was he to stand in the way of her rejoicing? He could not keep one thought from running around inside his mind. Though he knew her well enough to know that Robin had not intentionally left him out, she had not once referred to God in their conversation.

She left to talk again with Jerry before leaving for home. John stayed in the waiting room outside the ICU knowing he should be heading home himself. The doors opened again and Jerry's doctor came out with a chart in his hand, walking purposely toward the elevator. When he saw John sitting alone he turned and sat in the chair Robin had just vacated.

"I've seen you here visiting other patients. Ever had anything like this happen before?"

John had noticed over the years of visiting people in the hospital that doctors spoke with a minimum of words and often without any context or introduction.

"Not like this, no. I've prayed for lots of people, and a lot got better, but no, nothing like this."

"I didn't believe it when the X ray came back negative, showing the tumor was gone. So I did a complete body scan, thinking for whatever reason the cancer may have gone somewhere else. It doesn't make any medical sense, but neither does the tumor suddenly vanishing."

The doctor was tired as well and took a minute to collect his thoughts before he spoke again.

"I've seen a few things I couldn't understand over the years, but nothing like this. She says you prayed for him to be healed, is that right?"

"I wasn't the only one."

"But she says you're the only one who really believed he was going to be healed. I talked to our chaplain this evening when it became clear what happened. He told me he has prayed for thousands of people and can't ever remember anyone being healed who was so near death. Do you know something that he doesn't?"

All John knew at that moment was God had responded to his prayer and healed Jerry. John knew on some level he believed God would do the miraculous, but he was as unprepared for it as the doctor who was asking him if he had a direct line to God. He surprised himself when he said something he had spoken before.

"I have prayed for Jerry to be healed. I guess that's all I can say."

He wasn't exaggerating; he really couldn't say anything else. He was tired and he was still coming to terms with what happened. All he saw were unintended consequences he could not have imagined when he asked for God to heal Jerry. John wanted to share in the happiness that Robin had found, but it just wasn't there yet. Maybe tomorrow when he had a chance to sleep.

The doctor nodded as if he understood, and then rose from the chair. He turned and walked away to the elevator and said to John as he pushed the button,

"Your world is never going to be the same."

The last thing that happened to John in the waiting room was his phone ringing for the second time that evening. It was Sharon, probably wondering where he had gone. He answered her call and before she could speak he told her Robin had called and wanted him to come to the hospital right away. He listened for a moment and then said,

"No. It's just the opposite."

2

Friday 12.30 am

Things did not become any clearer for John as he drove home. One part of him was coming to the realization that God had done a great thing by healing Jerry. John realized for reasons unknown to him at the moment, God had decided to answer his prayer. He was drained physically and emotionally but could still feel both thankful and amazed at what God had done. As he turned into his driveway and saw the lights on he knew the night was not over. Sharon would be the first one he would talk with about what happened to Jerry. He wondered where the conversation would go.

She was waiting for him in the living room, sitting on the couch drinking a cup of coffee. Before he sat down he asked,

"Is there more coffee?"

"Yes. Why don't you sit down and I'll get you some."

He sat down across from the couch and waited for her to return. When she came back from the kitchen he took the cup from her and had a small sip. It was past midnight and he doubted he would get much sleep that night.

"So tell me what's happened."

"The short version is that Jerry's tumor is gone. He began feeling better this morning and an x ray confirmed that it's just not there. They're going to wait one day and if nothing changes he'll go home tomorrow."

"You're saying he's healed from his tumor. There's no other explanation?"

He didn't blame her for looking for another explanation, he might have said the same thing if he was in her position.

"I had a chance to talk to the doctor and he was very convincing. I don't think he would let Jerry go home if there was any doubt."

Sharon sat quietly on the couch, thinking the thing through. In her work as a paralegal she was used to researching facts and arguments to help build a case for the lawyers she worked for. In this case she had to look beyond what was normal into the realm of faith, a place where despite her background, she was not comfortable.

"You haven't answered my question. You're saying he was healed, right?"

"Yes. That's what I am saying."

"Because you prayed for him?"

"I prayed that God would heal Jerry and help him become a believer. It seems half of that prayer is answered. Not the most important half if you ask me."

Like John, Sharon had never seen anyone healed who was so near death and considered terminal. She had not spent weeks like John thinking about how God works and why he does or does not answer prayer. But she did have one thought which she shared with him. A thought that came from years of living with her father.

"God must be pleased with you to answer such a big prayer."

Despite his tiredness, despite the hour, despite the fog developing in his brain; he saw the opening and he took it.

"I don't think this has anything to do with how God feels about me. I certainly didn't do anything special to make him heal Jerry. In fact, I have no idea why God healed Jerry except that he wanted to."

Though Sharon had never told anyone, she knew God was not pleased with her. The reasons in her mind were endless and the proof was in the fact that he had denied her a child. A child that she did and did not want. It was late, and she was as tired as John, which explains what she said next. She said the words to herself, thinking back over a life where she felt she had never met the expectations either her father or God.

"If I couldn't please my father, how could I ever please God?"

John thought for a moment before he responded. He wanted to say the right thing because she had never said anything like this before.

"I don't know how your father feels about you, but I do know how God feels about you. I can assure you that you don't have to do anything to please him. Unlike your father, God has no conditions you have to meet to be accepted by him. You know Jesus did all that for you."

When he talked about her dad, he said the wrong thing and he knew it. It was too much to drop on her at once and he knew he wasn't the right one to talk about her relationship to him. He was more than a little surprised when she said,

"I don't think my father has any feelings for me, but I suspect that you already knew that."

"You don't think that your father loves you?"

"I didn't say that. I said that I don't think he has any feelings for me. But then he probably doesn't have any feelings for anybody."

He was expecting something much different, so he didn't know immediately how to respond. The spell was broken when she got up and walked down the hall to the bedroom. He sat in the chair to let her have a few minutes to herself. A door had opened briefly, one that he didn't even know existed, and it had shut just as quickly. How he would open it again he could not see and he did not know what he would say when it opened. It would turn out that someone else would open the door and discover things in Sharon's life that had never seen the light of day.

3

She was gone when he finally woke up the next morning. He slept until 9 and while lying in bed thought about what the day was going to look like. He decided he would wait until later in the afternoon to go back to the hospital to see Jerry. John had set up a meeting with Edward at 11 to make an official offer of employment. He had the board's blessing and wanted to get Edward hired and working as soon as possible. Though it was a thought hidden below the surface, John wanted something new going on at the church to balance out what was sure to be a time dominated by what happened to Jerry.

By the time he got to his office Susan had been there for nearly an hour. The phone had not stopped ringing. Several people in the church worked at the hospital where word had spread about the man who was healed from a brain tumor. Those who called either wanted more information or wanted to talk to John. He was expecting this and asked Susan to tell people he would talk about what happened in church that Sunday. Susan, however, would not be so easily put off. When John had time to settle into his office she knocked on the door, and then let herself in.

"One of the calls you got this morning was from Robin. She would like you to call her when you get a chance. How is she doing? She must be on cloud nine."

"I think that's one way to describe it. She probably didn't get much sleep last night. I know I didn't."

"Do you think Jerry will be at church Sunday? After what's happened I would think he would be the first one through the door."

"I haven't talked to Jerry yet so I don't know what he's thinking. I plan on heading over to the hospital later today and see how he's doing. He's the object of a lot of attention right now. I'm not sure that's a good thing, but it probably can't be helped. You have to remember, just because someone experiences a miracle doesn't necessarily mean they will believe God did it. Remember the passage in Luke that says some people won't believe even if they see a person raised from the dead."

"But this happened to Jerry. What other explanation can there be? I would think that he would be grateful to the person who believed God was going to heal him."

There was no way John could keep this from in some manner being about him. Because he told people he had prayed for Jerry to be healed, and had a certainty about him when he spoke, some were going to think of him as the instrument God used to heal Jerry. Try as he might to minimize his role in this, it was just not going to happen.

"I wasn't the only one who prayed for Jerry. You have to remember that."

"Of course. We all understand that it was God who did this. But you were the only one who really believed it would happen."

John wanted to reply, Then what does that say about everyone else? But he knew he was in that group too, and was still trying to figure out what part his faith had to do with what happened to Jerry. Instead he said,

"Well, let's get back to work and let this sort itself out. Once Jerry gets home and back in a normal routine we can see what's going to happen with him. We should still pray for him to be converted. That's the bigger issue for him and for us."

"Yes, that's true", she said, though her heart wasn't in it. Like nearly everyone else, it was the healing that captured her attention. The phone rang yet again and Susan left John's office to answer it at her desk. She returned moments later somewhat out of breath and handed him a message form with a phone number on it.

"It's from channel 4. They want to talk to you."

It had not entered his mind that the news media would become part of the story. He would find out later that Jerry's doctor was married to one of the local news anchors. John took the message from Susan and sat it on his desk. He was not going to return the call and hoped they would lose interest if he did not respond. When he didn't immediately reach for the phone to return the call, Susan said,

"This could be good for the church. You know what they say, that's there no bad publicity."

He wasn't going to go on television and talk about something that he didn't completely understand and could be used as a sideshow. John didn't see how anything good could come from letting any form of media become a part of the story. Then he thought of Robin. If they had reached out to him they certainly would reach out to her as well. The young mother whose husband had been brought back from certain death and restored to his family. He picked up the phone and before he began to dial Robin's number he said to Susan,

"Thanks for the message. I'm going to call Robin back and see how she's doing."

Susan knew this was a signal for her to leave and she shut the door behind her as she returned to her desk. As John waited for Robin to answer he saw another incoming call light up the phone and thought it was going to be a long day. Robin didn't answer so he left a brief voicemail asking her to call him on his cell phone. He didn't know what he would say; he just didn't want her to become a way to boost ratings for a television station.

John had an hour until his appointment with Edward and knew he was not going to get anything done until then. He got up from his desk and walked out from his office past Susan and into the hallway. The auditorium was to his left and he moved to one of the doors and went inside. He walked past the rows of chairs and sat down on the edge of the stage. He had never thought about what would happen if God answered his prayer. John understood now that his motives were mixed, as both Robert and Amy had observed. He wanted Jerry healed; there was no doubt about that. He also knew he wanted God to do something big. Why he wanted that he wasn't sure, but Robert's words to him that he was in a difficult place personally kept coming back to him. He didn't feel he was in a difficult place, yet here he was sitting alone in a semi dark auditorium trying to avoid the consequences of what he had set in motion by believing God would do something miraculous.

He had the faith to believe that God would do something big; did he have the faith to believe God was bigger than the events swirling around him? What did God want him to do now that Jerry was healed? John thought about the healings in the book of Acts. They were not kept secret, they were done out in the open for everyone to see. The apostles didn't apologize when God did something big; they seemed to expect he would do big things. John was the one who thought the board was putting God in a box of their own making, taking him out when needed and then putting him back. Well, God was out of the box now, and John was not going to put him back.

He returned to his office and looked at the message from the television news anchor. John dialed the number and waited for someone to answer. It turned out the number was the cell phone of the news anchor. She did not answer and he left a message asking her to call him when she had a chance. She would not return his call until later that day. She didn't return his call because she was spending time with Robin, who was telling her how John's prayer had healed her husband.

4

Friday 11.00 am

Edward arrived promptly at 11 and waited in Susan's office. John was talking with Wayne on the phone, who called when he heard from a friend who worked at the hospital that Jerry was healed. Wayne was excited and like Susan was thinking how this was going to affect the church. He also had kind words for John, telling him that he was proud of him as his pastor for hanging in there and believing God would heal Jerry. John mostly listened as Wayne talked, then thanked him for calling, letting him know he had an appointment.

Susan was the first one to tell Edward about Jerry. He listened as Susan told him what she knew. She told him about all the calls from people wanting more information and of the television station wanting to speak with John. Edward asked her how she thought this might affect the church. Susan responded positively, saying that it would undoubtedly bring people to visit the church; that could only be a good thing. Edward nodded his head, keeping his thoughts to himself. After a few minutes John opened the door and motioned for him to come inside.

When they were both seated, John asked Edward if Susan had told him about Jerry. Edward nodded and waited for John to respond.

"I know this is going to dominate things here at the church for the next several days. I want to offer you the position and begin thinking about what the next several months will look like."

"How is the family handling this? Have you had time to talk with them about what's happened?"

"I talked with Robin last night at the hospital and have tried to reach her today. I'm going to head over to the hospital later this afternoon and see how Jerry's doing. I don't have any idea what he's thinking about any of this."

"And how are you doing? I imagine you didn't get a lot of sleep last night."

John again was struck that it was Edward who was asking the questions and leading the conversation. Edward had just been offered the job he was seeking and yet had not made any reference to it. He seemed to be more concerned about what was happening to Robin, Jerry and John.

"I'm still coming to grips with everything. I feel like I'm still catching up emotionally. It's funny, but I never thought about what it would look like if Jerry was healed. Now I'm finding out."

Though John had used the word "if" in referring to Jerry being healed, Edward didn't think that it reflected any doubt on whether John thought Jerry was going to be healed. He had seen John before the board convinced God would heal Jerry. Edward knew from his own experience that the reality could be very different than the belief.

"You might also think about how this is going to affect the church. Something like this doesn't happen every day. And it's certainly going to last more than a few days. For you, this is going to last the rest of your life. You're going to be known as the pastor who beat cancer."

They still had not talked about the job offer John was presenting to Edward. John wanted a respite from talking about Jerry; he wanted something that day to be normal. He also thought that Edward was comparing what happened to him in Mexico with what was happening to John. He said to Edward,

"How much of this is coming from what happened to you with the man who was healed in Mexico? I know that wasn't a positive experience for you but that doesn't mean it will be the same in this case."

"I never said it wasn't a positive experience. I just told you what happened. It certainly was positive for the man who was healed. And perhaps for the church as well. I learned that when God works it's going to be messy and have consequences that you can't foresee."

John recognized that Edward was echoing the same thought he had; that if by faith you let God out of the box events could take on a life of their own. Edward wasn't finished yet, and added,

"You remember in the Chronicles of Narnia. When Mr. Beaver refers to Aslan as a wild lion. Not like a tame one. You have prayed that God would do something big and he has. That bigness is going to wash over a lot of people before this is done."

"I think God is big enough to get us through whatever comes, don't you?"

"Certainly. This could be a great opportunity for people to understand how great God is. It could also be a rock that causes people to stumble. You'll just have to wait and see. I hope you're up to the challenge."

John didn't appreciate the fact that Edward was giving him advice. He thought Edward would accept his offer; they would talk about introducing him to the church and then have him begin to work on a plan to get small groups going. In every conversation he had with Edward it had not gone as he anticipated. He wondered what their working relationship would be like if every conversation was like this. He wasn't thrilled at the prospect.

Edward knew he had pushed the envelope with John but wanted him to know what he was thinking. He valued honesty and hoped John did as well. Edward was willing to do whatever John asked him as his boss, but also thought John needed to know he was not shy about speaking what he saw as the truth.

"I hope you don't mind that I've been a little free with you. I want you to know that I respect the fact that you're the leader of the church. But you also need to know I'm not afraid to say what I feel. I hope that's not going to be a problem. I think we could work well together."

John thought Edward was wrong about the influence Jerry's healing would have on the church. He was convinced that the attention it was now generating would eventually subside and allow things in his world to return to normal. He could not have been more wrong.

"It's not going to be a problem, trust me."

5

John agreed to meet with the news anchor from channel 4 after he visited with Jerry in the hospital. His one condition was they meet in his office at the church. As he drove to the hospital he thought about what he wanted to say to Jerry. John knew Robin had told Jerry that   John was in some way responsible for his tumor disappearing. The first thing John wanted to do was convince Jerry that God healed him. He hoped it would open a door into Jerry's heart so he would come to believe. In what would be considered the greatest of ironies, instead of mentally planning Jerry's funeral John was now thinking how he was going to integrate Jerry into the life of the church when he became a Christian.

Robin was not there when John arrived at Jerry's room. The excitement and energy from last night had dissipated as people got used to the fact of Jerry's healing. There wasn't anyone in the room. Jerry was sitting upright watching television. The only reminder of what happened the night before was when the nurse who let him into the ICU greeted John by calling him "miracle man". He had smiled weakly and let it pass. When Jerry saw him through the glass walls coming toward his room he turned the television off and waved him in. John spoke first.

"I'm sorry I didn't get a chance to talk with you last night. It was busy in here. How are you feeling?"

John again noticed there were no tubes, no IV lines, no wires and no monitors attached to Jerry. The doctors must have looked him over again since yesterday and obviously had not found anything. Jerry's skin, which just days ago was sallow and pale, now glowed pink and he seemed the fountain of health. John couldn't think of any reason why he wouldn't leave the hospital tomorrow.

"I'm feeling much better, thanks. The doctor says I can go home tomorrow. And back to work next week. It's all happened so fast it's kind of hard to believe."

"Even for those of us who prayed for this to happen it's hard to believe. Sometimes when God does something big we're all caught off guard."

John wanted to introduce God into the conversation as soon as possible. He was hoping Jerry would recognize what happened to him was the result of God's direct intervention in his life.

"Yeah, I want to thank you for your prayers. Robin is convinced that you played a part in what's happened. The doctor doesn't know how to explain it, but it really doesn't matter to me. I'm just glad I can go back to my family."

John ran Jerry's words back through his mind. Robin is convinced. The doctor doesn't know how to explain it. It was clear Jerry at that point didn't care how his tumor had disappeared, he was just happy that it was gone. John did not see the wisdom in trying to convince Jerry right then and there that he should fall on his knees and thank God for healing him. But he wasn't ready to give up quite yet.

"It's not every day you get to witness a miracle. I know Robin and the kids have faithfully prayed that you would get better. Lots of people at our church have prayed for you as well. I'm sure glad I won't have to come visit you in the hospital anymore."

Before Jerry could answer, his doctor came into the room looking down at the chart he had taken from outside the door. When he saw John sitting by Jerry's bed he said,

"Good morning pastor. Come to visit your miracle I see."

It should not have surprised John that the doctor spoke sarcastically to him. In ways that the doctor would not admit, the disappearance of Jerry's tumor had made him seem smaller to the staff on the ICU and even in his own eyes. He told them Jerry did not have long to live and here he was about to be discharged from the hospital. The doctor could not explain it, and knew that most of the nurses credited the pastor for Jerry's healing. Doctors generally looked on clergy as low paid comforters who guided families through the grief process, not healers who could conquer disease.

Jerry was clearly embarrassed by what the doctor said, caught as he was between two different sets of beliefs and values. He really didn't care how he got better, and did not like being referred to as a "miracle". He felt the tension in the room and tried to diffuse it by saying,

"Hey doc, do I still get to go home tomorrow?"

"It looks that way. I'm going to take you down one more time for an X ray and if it's still clear you can leave tomorrow."

He had put emphasis on the word "if", implying that he would not be surprised if the tumor magically showed up again in Jerry's brain. John's presence in the room had clearly thrown him off his game. At that moment an orderly appeared at the door with a gurney to take Jerry down to X ray. Jerry looked at the gurney and said,

"I don't think I need any help getting to x ray. I've been walking around the floor all morning. Why don't I just walk with the orderly?"

The doctor was not about to let a patient tell him about hospital policy.

"You'll have plenty of time for walking when you leave. Let's abide by hospital policy while you're here."

He spoke with an air of finality that allowed no debate. John had to move so the orderly could get in the room with the gurney. He decided it would be a good time to leave. He said to Jerry in parting,

"I'll see you soon. Say" hi" to Robin and the kids."

The doctor had to have the last word. As John walked past him the doctor said,

"Good luck with my wife this afternoon."

John paused and looked at the doctor, who had his back turned to him. He wanted to respond but thought better of it. He didn't know what the doctor meant, but his tone was definitely condescending and sarcastic. He wanted to shout to the man that it was God who reached into Jerry's brain and took out the tumor when the doctor was powerless to do anything. It was rare for John to get upset about anything, but he was just at the point of letting go when a nurse touched him gently on the shoulder. She could see he was visibly upset and heard some of the conversation from the doorway.

"He's not worth it, believe me."

She guided him out of the room and walked with him down the hallway to the door. John regretted the fact the nurse could see he was upset. He had gone to the hospital with only one goal in mind and was leaving without having accomplished anything with Jerry. And what had the doctor meant when he talked about John meeting with his wife? His thoughts were interrupted when they came to the ICU door. The nurse pushed the button that opened the large door and said to John as he left the ICU,

"Don't worry about him. He's just jealous. We all know what happened here."

"What do you think happened here?"

"You healed him, that's what happened."

It wouldn't be the last time he would hear someone say that exact same phrase, a phrase that would haunt him over the next several days.

6

Friday 5.30 pm

John had a chance to collect himself as he drove back to the church. His day was certainly not turning out the way he envisioned. First there was the growing reality that in some minds the healing was going to be about him. As much as this thought disturbed him, he knew he could not change how people were going to think. Then there was Edward. He wasn't exactly throwing cold water on what had happened, but brought words of caution to a situation that screamed out for rejoicing.

The biggest letdown was with Jerry. There wasn't any other explanation for his cure except God healed him, yet he didn't want to acknowledge that as a possibility. At least not yet. John had enough experience working with people to know that conversion was usually a process and not a dramatic event. He also knew some of the people Jesus healed did not believe in him even though they could feel in their bodies the evidence of him being the Son of God. What would be the point of God healing Jerry if he didn't believe?

Then there was the doctor. He was clearly antagonistic toward John, and though he could understand why, what was the point of trying to humiliate him in front of Jerry? It was as if Jerry was an embarrassment to the doctor, something he couldn't explain. And why the parting remark about his wife? That the doctor and the news anchor were married was a surprise to him, had the doctor poisoned the well before John had a chance to speak with her? John agreed to meet with her in order to bring God into the public conversation as the reason for Jerry's healing. He tried to do that with Jerry and failed. Would the next time be any different?

They agreed to meet at 5.30 in John's office. He wanted Susan to be gone when he talked to the anchor so she would not be a distraction. John saw the news van pull into the parking lot and had a moment of panic. He silently prayed for wisdom in what to say and that he would not become the focus of the story. He got up and made his way to the front doors of the church and walked outside to greet the anchor and her cameraman, who were just getting out of the van. When she saw John she extended her hand, and with a smile said,

"You must be John. I'm so glad you took time to meet with us. My name is Julie."

He shook her hand and said,

"No problem. I just found out this morning your husband is Jerry's doctor. Small world."

"Yes it is. That's how I found out about what's happened, though I guess it's common knowledge at the hospital. Has any other media contacted you?"

"No. I hadn't thought about the media until you called the church this morning."

"Well, they will, trust me. We don't get stories like this very often. Stories that have a happy ending and a touch of the miraculous."

John would make sure he talked with her about the miraculous part of the story, no matter what else transpired. He would not have enough time to get a first impression of her and because he did not normally watch the local news, had no idea what she was like as an interviewer. John knew she would bring her own perspective and beliefs to the questions she asked, as well as what she thought would make her viewers interested in the story. He would do the same and had thought about different ways to make God and what he had done the focus of their time. As they walked into the lobby she said,

"If we can get started quickly this can make the 11 o'clock news."

"Sure, right this way."

It took about ten minutes to set up the camera and get the sound ready. She decided to have them both sit in front of his desk so they would both be in the shot. The cameraman would vary the viewpoint of the camera, sometimes on her and other times on John, depending on who was speaking. She explained all of this to John and asked if he was ready to begin.

"Just relax. You'll be fine. If we need to stop we can, okay?"

"How long do you think this will take?"

John noticed that her legal pad was covered with questions. When she saw him looking down at it she discreetly pulled it toward her so he could not see what was written.

"Only a few minutes. We try to keep the stories we chose to air to no more than five minutes."

"There's a chance this won't be on the air?"

"Not this story. It's already being promoted on the shows leading up to the news."

She nodded to the cameraman and when he signaled he was ready with his thumb up, she said to John,

"Here we go."

Her first questions were innocent enough. She asked about the church, his background and how long he had known Robin and Jerry. She had him describe his relationship with the family and the progress of Jerry's disease. John was able to answer these first questions with short answers and kept waiting for a place to talk about what happened to Jerry. Then she said,

"How many people have you healed in your ministry?"

He was ready for this question, but not for the ones that followed.

"I want to make it clear that I haven't healed anyone. There were any number of people praying that God would do this. Sometimes the more public figure gets the attention, but in this case it was truly a team effort. We asked and God answered."

"So I take it that Jerry is the first person you've prayed for who has been healed in what we could call a dramatic fashion?"

She had probably picked that up from Robin, he thought.

"His has certainly been the most dramatic, yes. But like I've said, our whole church has been praying for this family."

"I think you're being modest. When I talked with Robin this afternoon she made it clear that you were the one who believed her husband was going to be healed. Isn't that true?"

It was true, but he knew he couldn't answer that way. It would set him apart from everyone else, which was the very thing he was trying to avoid.

"I think we're missing the point that God did something big here. There isn't any other explanation for this. I would think that would be the story."

She ignored what he said and followed with another question.

"What would you do if other people came to you for prayer? Would you pray for them to be healed as well?"

He couldn't really say he wasn't in the healing business; that would minimize what happened to Jerry. He also couldn't say that not every prayer for healing was answered as dramatically as this one; that would seem to minimize God. John decided the best thing to do was just to tell the truth but not directly answer her question.

"I don't always understand why God heals some and not others. But I do trust that he knows what he's doing. And I know that it's never wrong to ask him to do things for us."

"But isn't it true that God uses people to accomplish his purposes?"

"Yes. It's true that God uses people. He has used a number of us in this case."

"But why do you think Robin would say that it was your prayer that healed Jerry?"

John now knew why the doctor made the remark about his wife. She came to this interview to make John the story; not Jerry, not Robin and certainly not God. The pastor who prays for people and they are healed.

"I think she's just looking at the person she's had the most contact with. I'm just glad that God has given her husband back to her."

"Again, I think you're being too modest."

That was it, the interview was over. She accomplished what she wanted and needed to get the tape back to the station to air that evening. She put her legal pad in her bag and thanked John for his time. She told him she thought it had gone well. He did not share her opinion but kept his thoughts to himself.

He walked with them out the front door of the church to the news van, exactly one hour after they had arrived. John knew she was probably completely oblivious to the fact that by making him the center of the story she had done exactly what he had feared. In her world people wanted to be the story so why would John be any different? She tried to give him special powers when all he wanted was to have her report that it was God's power that was displayed in Jerry. He didn't think of himself as particularly naïve about how the world worked, but he wouldn't know that from what just happened.

7

Saturday 8.00 am

John wanted to visit Robin and Jerry at home some time on
Saturday but it was not possible. Jerry came home that morning
and when John talked to Robin about coming over she said it was
too early. Jerry needed time to adjust to being out of the hospital.
Sharon had to work on a huge case that her office was about to
litigate, so John had the whole day to himself.

He was not going to go to the office; he needed a break from the
phone ringing all the time. Since Jerry's healing became more widely
known in the church and now the community, people were
clamoring to speak with him. In just over twenty-four hours his
world had turned upside down. He had yet to speak with any of his
board members, all of whom left messages on his cell phone. There
were other media outlets who had called the church after they saw the
news report Friday night. There was even a call from the regional
director of his denomination.

John did not want to return any calls or set up any appointments
until he thought through what had happened and how to get ahead
of the events that were unfolding. Foremost in his mind was getting
another opportunity to talk with Jerry before his life returned to
normal and the immediacy of his healing wore off. His primary
reason for wanting God to heal Jerry, at least what he was telling
himself, was that he wanted Jerry's life spared so he could believe.
John also wanted Robin to experience God dramatically intervening

in her husband's life so her faith would be strengthened. He also did not want the children to lose their dad and become fatherless at such a young age.

John also needed to think about what he was going to say to the church on Sunday. Most of the church would have heard by Sunday morning about the healing. They would be expecting a word from their pastor, who was at the center of the story. Some of them would have seen the story on the 11 o'clock news. They would need him to provide some context for a story that basically said he was the reason Jerry was healed. Then there was the newspaper.

He seldom looked at the newspaper, but Sharon read it every day. John brought the newspaper in that morning and sat it on the kitchen table without bothering to glance at the front page. When Sharon sat down at the table with her coffee, she looked at the front page and saw the article on the bottom fold. She quickly read it and then said to John, who was seated across from her,

"Did you talk to the newspaper about Jerry?'

"I haven't talked to anybody except the anchor from channel 4. I turned my phone off before that and haven't turned it back on yet."

Then he understood why she asked.

"You mean there's an article in the paper about this?"

"See for yourself."

She handed him the paper and he quickly read the article. As he read the copy it seemed to accurately report what happened. They stated they were not able to get in touch with the pastor but had quotes from one of the nurses, the hospital chaplain and then, to his consternation, Susan. How they found her he could only wonder. As he read what she said he had to fight to keep his temper in check. She told how he believed all along Jerry was going to be healed, how compassionate he was and how lucky the church was to have him as their pastor.

Sharon was watching him as he became visibly upset and could guess the reason.

"You ought to give her a raise. She certainly went out of her way to increase your profile in the community. I'm sure looking forward to seeing what church is like tomorrow, aren't you?"

"She means well, but she's naïve. She's thinking this will give the church more visibility and bring in lots of new people. She doesn't understand that I don't want this to be about me. She's just adding fuel to the fire."

"If you ask me, that ship has sailed and you're at the helm. I wish I could stay but I have to get to work. Don't worry, this too shall pass."

"That's not what Edward thinks."

He had told her about hiring Edward, but not much else about him. She responded by asking,

"What does he know about this?"

"More than you think."

Moments later she was out of the house and on her way to work. John thought for a moment about the best way to spend the day. Eventually he would have to check his phone and at least return those calls that he thought important. First he would send an email to the board and at least let them know he was aware they were trying to contact him. He went into his study and turned on his computer. John thought about what he wanted to say while it booted up. When it was ready to go, this is the email he sent:

It was late Thursday night that I was contacted by Robin to come immediately to the hospital. There I found that Jerry's tumor was gone, something we had been praying about for a long time. Since then I seem to be playing catch-up to what has happened. I have talked to both Robin and Jerry. Jerry went home today and seems completely recovered. This is a great answer to prayer and we should rejoice. My biggest concern is that I have become a larger part of this story than I desire. I know that's somewhat inevitable, but I still find it awkward. Would you pray Jerry would realize that it was God who healed him and that I would have wisdom in how to deal with this in the coming days? Let's talk next week. I'll let you know about a time.

As much as he was dreading it, he turned on his phone and looked to see how many messages there were. Before he could even look at the voicemail screen, the phone rang. It was Robert, a call he was willing to take.

"Robert, how are you? I guess you've heard?"

"Yeah, I saw the news last night. I'm guessing it's been a long couple of days."

"Yes it has, to say the least. I wasn't quite prepared for all this. You're the first person I've talked with since this happened."

"Except for the television reporter."

"Yeah. Except for her. And Sharon."

"You happy with the way that turned out?"

"What? You mean the interview?"

"Of course the interview. This is becoming about you, is that what you want?"

"I'm trying to do the exact opposite. You'll remember I kept trying to give God the credit. It wasn't my fault that she kept coming back to me."

"Well what did you think she was going to do, let you do a five minute commercial for how great God is? She can't interview God, she can't ask him questions, but she can take a run at you and make you the story. You're lucky she wanted to make you the story and not destroy you in the process, which she could have easily done."

John didn't like someone else pointing out what had become obvious to him and did not immediately respond.

"You still there?"

"Yeah I'm still here, but you're not telling me anything I don't already know. What I need is some advice on how to proceed. I have to say something to my church tomorrow."

"My best advice would be take a two week vacation and get away from all of this, but I don't suppose that's possible."

"No it's not possible, and that's not really advice is it?"

"No, I suppose not. How is the family doing?"

"Well, the wife is overjoyed she got her husband back. The only downside is that the one time I've got to speak with the husband he doesn't seem to care God healed him. He's just glad that he's better."

"So you got your answer but it hasn't turned out the way you expected, is that about right?"

"Yes, that's about right. I'm thrilled at the result but I have no idea what this is going look like in the immediate future. I'm trying to find a way to get out of the spotlight."

"Good luck with that. If you can't make yourself scarce then make your words scarce. And I want to warn you, people will come out of the woodwork looking for you. And not for interviews."

"You're talking about people coming to me for healing?"

"Well what else would they come to you for? It's not every day you get someone who can beat cancer. I know you don't want to hear that, but that's what people are going to think."

"Anything I can do about that?"

"Not that I can think of at the moment."

"What would you do if you were me?"

"I don't see how you can turn people away if they come to you. Just be honest and say you don't know why God healed Jerry, you're just thankful that he did. If you ask me, it's you board your have to worry about."

"My board, why would they be a problem?"

"They're probably not going to understand any of this. They have certain expectations regarding church and I can tell you that healing people is not one of them. Your denomination is generally conservative in areas like this. They'll probably be happy that one person is healed, but if you let the cat out of the bag they're just going to want to put it back in."

John desperately wanted to change the subject. He felt if he kept talking he would get in a hole he could not crawl out of. He asked Robert,

"Are you ready for your surgery? How are you feeling?"

"I wouldn't need the surgery if you prayed for me, would I?"

"Really, this isn't a situation that calls for humor, is it?"

"Sorry, couldn't help myself. Yeah, I'm as ready as I can be. You're welcome to attend if you wish."

"I'll be there. Robert, please pray for me. I'm going to need it."

"Yes you are. More than you know."

8

Sunday 7 am

John arrived at church Sunday morning just as dawn was breaking. He wanted a few hours alone before he faced his congregation. He was not going to change the service and would only at the end speak about Jerry. The one thought that encouraged him was he would be able to say what he wanted, the way he wanted and for as long as he wanted. The biggest unknown that morning was how many visitors they might have as a result of the story getting out in the media. It had just been over 48 hours since Jerry was healed and the story had been in both the newspaper and on the television. As he sat in his office he had to admit he had no idea what was going to happen.

He hoped Jerry would attend but knew that would bring him attention that he certainly would not want. The last thing John wanted was for Jerry to be self-conscious when he came to church, but how was he going to stop that? John knew people would want to talk to him about his healing and how happy they were for him and Robin.

Finally, he just gave up and decided that if God was big enough to heal Jerry he was big enough to handle what would happen that morning. He thought again about what he had told the board. John told them that once you let God out of the box it was hard to put him back. John realized that he did not want to put God back into the box and was willing to go wherever he led. Would others be willing to follow?

John met each Sunday morning before the service with the worship team to go over the order of service and bring up any last minute concerns. As John walked from his office to the rehearsal room where he would meet with them he could hear the sound of people coming into the lobby from the outside. The service was going to start in 30 minutes; usually it was quiet in the lobby at this hour. He opened the door into the rehearsal room and smiled as he greeted them. Before he could go over the order of service, the band leader said,

"Looks like there's going to be a lot of people today."

"I suspect we'll have a number of visitors today. I think most of you have heard what's happened to Jerry. His tumor is gone and he went home yesterday. It's a huge answer to our prayers and we'll have to see what else God is going to do. I would like to make one change this morning."

John usually did the opening welcome and announcements before the service started but did not want to speak today until it was time for his message. He asked the worship leader to do the welcome and said they would skip the announcements that morning. John was positive, encouraging and asked his team to pray for him as he spoke to the church. Then he prayed and they walked out into the auditorium.

On a normal Sunday they averaged around 250 people. There was seating for 300 and extra chairs stored in a utility room down the hallway. When John stepped into the auditorium, he saw that nearly all of the seats were taken. There were men bringing more chairs into the room, but John knew immediately they would not be able to seat everyone. The auditorium was approved by the fire department for 300. It was obvious to him there was going to more than 300 who wanted to attend.

He resisted the urge to take control of the situation and decided to let the ushers and greeters figure out what to do. With twenty minutes until the service began he did not want to be in the auditorium. People would want to talk with him and he wanted everyone to hear at the same time what he had to say about Jerry. He turned and went back to the rehearsal room and sat down, intending to look over the notes of his message.

Before he could even pull the notes from his Bible, Michael, who had seen him walk into the auditorium and then back to the rehearsal room, stepped in through the closed door. As soon as he shut the door he said,

"Have you seen how many people are out there? What are we going to do?"

There was a note of panic in his voice, no doubt triggered by thoughts like, Where are we going to put all these people? What if the Fire Marshall shows up? What is John going to say? Who are all of these people? What do they want? What is going to happen?

"Yes, I have. It looks like it's going to be standing room only today."

"We're not going to have enough seats, you know that."

"Then I guess some people are either going to have to stand or sit on the floor. It's a problem lots of churches would like to have. We'll be better prepared next week."

"You know why they're here."

"I'm hoping they're here because they heard God has done a great thing. I'm hoping they came because they're curious about God and what he might do for them. Maybe they came because they think something might happen to them. At this point all we know is that God answered a prayer and this seems to be the result."

"What are you going to say to them?"

"I'm going to preach my regular message. After that I don't quite know what I'm going to say but I know I have to talk about Jerry. You should pray that God would give me the right words."

"Like you did with the news reporter for channel 4?"

"That's why you need to pray. I would like this to be about God and not me. This seems to be the only place I might be able to make that happen."

Michael was not a bad person; he was just way out of his depth. Where John saw opportunity, he saw problems. Where John saw a chance for God to work, he saw a situation that was out of control. John saw a mess, and wanted to walk towards it. Michael saw a mess and wanted to find a way to clean it up.

They began the service five minutes early since every seat was taken. There were a number of people standing against the outside walls and even more milling around the lobby. The greeters were now setting up chairs in the lobby and leaving the doors to the auditorium open so people could hear. The ushers decided to ask regular members of the church to move to the fellowship hall and listen there. This somewhat helped with the crowding but also meant that more than half of the people in the auditorium were visitors.

When John got up to speak he acknowledged the large number of visitors. He explained that after the message he would speak for a few minutes on another topic he guessed they were all aware of. John was in the middle of a series on building healthy relationships; that morning he spoke about honesty and the importance of telling the truth. He could tell the audience was listening, but there was also an expectation about what he was going to do after the message. He had been looking at faces for ten years as a speaker, and knew that most of them were waiting for him to finish and get to the main act.

He was done just before noon and then walked down from the stage to the floor of the auditorium. John knew that some would have a more difficult time seeing him, but wanted to be more personal in his demeanor. If Jerry and Robin had come, he did not see them. Most of the people he was looking at were strangers and were waiting expectantly for him to speak. He began by thanking everyone for coming, and then said,

"I know the main reason many of you have come today is because you heard that a man whose wife attends this church was healed of cancer. It's true, three days ago he was dying from a brain tumor and now that tumor is gone and he's returned home. Though many of us prayed for this man to be healed, I think few of us believed it would actually happen. But God has a way of turning up when we least expect it. I think God has shown it's never wrong to ask and that he's more than willing to do big, miraculous things in our lives. Do I think that God will heal every person that we pray for? No, I don't. But I now believe that it's not wrong to ask him to heal. Not only for our benefit, but more importantly to display God's power so people can turn to him in faith."

John paused for a moment, looked out over the auditorium, and then said,

"I know some of you came here today because you heard a miracle of healing had taken place. I know some of you came here to see if we would pray for you to be healed. I want you to understand that though God uses people to accomplish his purposes, I don't know God's will for anyone in this room. I only know it's not wrong to ask God to do big things in our lives. Finally, I suspect that many of you are not yet Christians. Whatever God does or does not do for you today, I want you to know that he loves you and wants you to believe in him for who he is, not just for what he will do for you."

For the next two hours, John prayed for people to be healed. He asked for those who wanted prayer for healing to stay and dismissed everyone else. About one hundred people stayed in the auditorium and waited in their seats while John moved among them. He asked each person their name and how he might pray for them. On some he laid his hands, for others he held their hand while he prayed. Many of those he prayed for wept as he asked God to be merciful to them and heal their sickness. Some left after he prayed for them, some stayed and sat quietly and watched as John worked his way through the room. Not everyone asked for physical healing. Some asked John to pray for difficult personal problems, some asked John to pray for financial resources and some asked John to just pray for them without giving him anything specific.

The fourth person that John prayed for was a man who saw the story on television Friday night. He had never been to church before. He had not been able to work due to a badly deteriorated hip. He had no insurance and was almost apologetic when he talked with John. He didn't have anywhere else to turn, so he thought he would give God a chance. He was extremely uncomfortable and kept apologizing for being there. John listened and then asked the man to stop. It was okay, John understood his concerns. John prayed for him, specifically asking for God to heal his hip so he could return to work. When he was finished, John said to the man,

"It's okay, you can leave now."

The man rose slowly from his seat and was ready to wince in pain as he usually did when getting up out of a chair. This time there was no pain. Even so he gingerly walked down the row of chairs to the aisle. When he reached the aisle he walked just a little faster, testing his hip to see how it would react. Those who were sitting next to him, who had listened to his conversation with John, watched as he left the auditorium. He would be back the next Sunday, walking into the church without a limp and without the cane he had used the last several months.

When John was almost done, he came to a woman who told him she could not have children. She attended another church in the city but read in the newspaper about the pastor who healed a man with terminal cancer. She felt God telling her to have John pray for her, though she had never experienced anything like that before. She was almost embarrassed as she spoke to John, who listened quietly. When she was done he didn't say anything for a few moments. Finally he took her hand and said,

"I don't need to pray for you. You're already pregnant. So let's thank God for that."

Then he moved on to the next person, leaving her alone with her thoughts. She watched as he prayed for the last few people, and then quietly rose and left the auditorium. It would turn out that her husband was not a Christian and thought going to John's church that morning was a bad idea. When she returned home much later than he anticipated, he told her he was worried and thought something may have happened to her. She told him what John said and when he expressed skepticism, she told him to sit down and wait. Returning a few minutes later with a smile on her face and a white plastic pregnancy test in her hand, she handed it gently to him. It was pink. The first thing Monday morning he called the church and made an appointment to see John. Thursday he became the first person to believe in God through the events that happened on Sunday. He would not be the last.

There was one other person who visited that morning who would make an appointment to see John that week. He stood in the back of the church, watching with interest, as John prayed for those in the auditorium. He had seen this before in different churches, and it brought back memories that were not pleasant. This time would be different, he thought.

9

Tuesday 10 am

This time they met at John's office. Mr. Banks wanted to meet as soon as possible, so John suggested he come by the office that day. John could not ever remember Mr. Banks calling him, let alone asking to meet. John had no idea what he wanted to talk about, but knew it must be important since what he was doing was so out of character.

John had a board meeting that night he had to prepare for and he was scheduled to meet with Edward later that day. Edward would begin work at the church the following week and John needed him to fill out the necessary paperwork. Mr. Banks was crowding his day and he wondered how long his visit would last. John didn't mind meeting with him but the memory of their last time together was not altogether pleasant.

He showed up right when he said he would. He parked his car and walked toward the front doors of the church. John could see he was again wearing a suit. This brought a smile to his face. It was just after 10 when he came into the outer office. He spoke briefly to Susan, who then rang John's phone.

Though it had only been a week since their last meeting, John noticed Mr. Banks looked older. Either that or he was worried about something. His face was drawn and there were dark circles under his eyes. It looked like he was not getting any sleep. When he came through the door John extended his hand in greeting. Mr. Banks responded, but John could see his heart was not in it. After Mr. Banks sat down John didn't wait to find out why he was there.

"Mr. Banks, I have to tell you that I'm a little surprised to see you. I can't remember the last time we saw each other twice in such a short time. What did you want to see me about"?

"Yes, well, I need your help."

"You need my help? With what exactly?"

John could not imagine a scenario where Mr. Banks would need his help for anything. Let alone ask. The room was quiet as John waited for Mr. Banks to respond. He would not look John in the eye and was sitting in the chair slowly wringing his hands. After a few moments of silence, John said,

"Mr. Banks?"

Finally, Mr. Banks straightened up and looked at John.

"I know you don't like me. I know you think that I'm out of touch and conservative to a fault. I know you think I was a terrible father and don't love my daughter. I want you to put all that aside if you can."

John was not going to disagree with him or say something like, No, that's not true at all. We just come from different generations. I know that you love your daughter. He had never heard Mr. Banks talk like this before. John knew from his years of counseling people it would be better if he didn't speak and let Mr. Banks continue. When John didn't respond and just kept looking at him, Mr. Banks continued.

"You don't know hard it is for me to come to talk with you. I wouldn't come if there was any other option. I want you to understand that."

John didn't know exactly how he was supposed to understand that remark. He doubted Mr. Banks would deliberately insult him when he wanted something from him. It was time to find out what was going on.

"Why did you come to see me?"

"My wife is ill."

"Yes, I know. The last time we met I asked you how she was doing and you didn't answer me. How is she doing?"

"She's dying. She's been ill for some time but now the doctors think she only has a few months left."

"I am so sorry. What is wrong with her, if I can ask?"

Mr. Banks looked out the window at the bright sunshine. Now that he had said the words he seemed to relax just a bit. As he spoke he continued to look outside and not at John, who thought he knew where the conversation was going.

"She has congestive heart failure. She's had it for several years. There really isn't anything they can do for her."

"Does Sharon know?"

"No. I have to tell her today, though her mother doesn't want me to."

It was typical of Sharon's mother to think that it would be a burden to her daughter if she knew her mother was dying. Instead of thinking Sharon might want to spend time with her, or possibly care for her, Mrs. Banks only thought was of how distressed her daughter might be if she knew. John thought he would spare Mr. Banks having to ask him the question that brought him to his office.

"You came here to ask me to pray for her to be healed."

"Yes. I did."

"How did you find out?"

John knew that Mr. Banks did not own a television and doubted he read the newspaper. John had no idea how Mr. Banks would have heard what happened to Jerry.

"I was at the market and glanced at the front page of the newspaper. There was an article about you. How you prayed for a man who had terminal cancer and he was healed."

John did not know how he was going to explain to Mr. Banks why God chose to heal Jerry. He would certainly pray for Mrs. Banks, but there was more at work here than what Mr. Banks was asking.

"You have to know that I'm not a miracle worker."

"The newspaper says otherwise."

There was just the slightest touch of firmness in Mr. Banks voice, a tone that said, Don't correct me when I know I'm right. When John prayed for people after the Sunday service, he knew it was right. He was confident God was in the room and knew some people had been touched by him and healed. Here all he felt was the desperation of a man running out of options.

"Mr. Banks, you need to go home and be with your wife. I'll pray that God comforts her and gives her peace." John paused for a moment, and then a thought occurred to him.

"Mr. Banks, you told me that God always hears your prayers. Even if the answer is no. Have you prayed for your wife to be healed?"

Mr. Banks was completely still, frozen to his chair. When he spoke it was in a whisper.

"I have, but God has not heard my prayer. I have displeased him and he has not heard my prayer." How he thought he displeased God, John would never know. Then he said to John,

"You're not going to pray for her to be healed?"

"Mr. Banks, what happens if I pray for your wife to be healed and she dies? You can't make me responsible for her life. It's not fair."

Mr. Banks wasn't done. If he couldn't persuade John, there was still one avenue left open to him. He rose from the chair and walked out of the office without a word, leaving the door open as he left. Susan watched him leave, and then knocked lightly on the open door.

"Who was that?"

"That was my father-in-law."

"I've never met him before, have I? What did he want? He seemed to leave in a hurry."

"Something that I couldn't provide. I doubt you'll ever see him here again."

10

Edward wasn't scheduled to meet John at his office until 2 p.m., so John left at noon and took his lunch to a local park. He wanted to sit in the sun and not have to think or talk to anyone for an hour or so. It was a bright, warm day and as he sat on a bench overlooking a small pond he could not get his mind to stop running in circles around the events of the last week.

For years he had been praying for different people: their needs, their circumstances, their trials and their temptations. Because he kept a list of those people, he was constantly reminded that most of what he prayed for went unanswered. Unless you viewed "no" as an answer. John was perfectly willing to accept that God would answer prayers with "no" or "not now". As the years went on, however, John knew it wasn't the fact that God wasn't saying "yes" that was bothering him, it was the fact when God finally said "yes", it only brought chaos into his life.

Everything was turned upside down; his conversation with Mr. Banks, the TV reporter and even Robert only highlighted the fact no one was giving God credit for what he had done. When John prayed for Jerry to be healed, his expectation was that Jerry would become a Christian. People would then marvel at God's power and it would help bring some momentum into the church. John had become a much bigger part of the story than he ever imagined and could not seem to get himself out of the way. He never expected people would start showing up at his church and want him to pray for them to be healed.

Then there was the board. He knew some of them would not be happy with what happened Sunday. John would have to answer their questions, explain himself and try to give them some idea what the future held. They were comfortable talking about budgets, programs, the building and anything that dealt with money. It was partly his fault; he had not led them into places where their faith or beliefs could be stretched. He had not shared with them any of his struggles with why God seemed to be silent to his prayers. Perhaps if he had they would be open to what God was doing.

Finally, there was Sharon. He was beginning to understand more about her from his conversation with Mr. Banks, his time with Amy and the conversation when Sharon talked about being a parent. What he always assumed was a disciplined, focused approach to her relationship with God; he was now seeing as an unhealthy desire to make God happy in the same way she tried to please her father. John understood he might not be the one who could help her see how foolish it was to think that God's love was conditioned on how she behaved.

He needed to get back to the office, but was reluctant to leave such a quiet, peaceful place. Because it was a weekday, there were few people in the park. Before he finished the last of his lunch, he spent a few minutes praying for the rest of his day. He wanted to be ready for the two meetings on his schedule and whatever else might come. When he was finished, he walked back to his car and took one last look around. It would be the last peaceful moment he would have for many days.

John thought the meeting with Edward would last long enough for him to fill out the necessary paperwork, talk about when he would begin and perhaps some small talk. However, Edward was always surprising him, something he wondered if he could adjust to.

It began when Edward asked about the Sunday service. He listened as John explained about the number of visitors and how they tried to accommodate them as best they could. Then he told Edward what he said after his message and how he invited those interested in prayer to remain after the service. He stopped for a moment as he thought back to what transpired in those two hours. Edward then asked,

"What happened then?"

"About a hundred people stayed. I spent two hours talking and praying for them. I have never experienced anything like that before. I know several people left having experienced either physical healing or some type of word from God."

"What are you planning for this week?"

"I don't know. I really didn't know what I was going to do Sunday until it happened. My thought was I couldn't send people away who came for prayer without praying for them."

"You mean people who came for healing?"

"Yes, I suppose that's why they came. You have to remember this all started because God answered a prayer for one man to be healed. I'm trying to follow God's leading here, and not do anything on my own."

"And where do you think God is leading?"

"Again, I don't know. But the fact that he healed several people last Sunday sort of confirms he might want us to continue to pray for people who show up here looking to be healed."

Edward was nodding his head as John spoke. John did not know if it was in agreement or just an acknowledgment he was following what he was saying. John was again playing catchup to Edward, so he quickly asked,

"Where are we going with these questions? Do you have a problem with anything I've done?"

"I'm wondering what kind of church I'll be working for. When we started this process your church was here and now it's moved here."

He held his hands about three feet apart to demonstrate for John his view of what happened at the church.

"Edward, like I've told you before, I'm just playing catchup here. I haven't planned anything; I haven't set anything in motion. I haven't changed what I believe. I'm just responding to something that God did in answer to a prayer."

John wished he was back in the park, in the warm sunshine and not having what seemed like the same conversation over and over. A conversation about the aftermath of something miraculous and not the miracle itself. He said as much to Edward.

"In the last three days all I have tried to do is give God credit for what he did and ask him to do the same for others. It doesn't seem like I'm having much success, does it?"

Edward felt genuinely sorry for John, but not in the way John might have imagined. Edward was thrilled that John experienced God breaking into his life with an answer to prayer that was truly miraculous and astounding. It would always be there for John to say, Look, God did something right here that cannot be explained except by his mighty power. Edward had that too, an experience of God doing something unexpected that could only be explained by the miraculous. Unlike John, however, Edward left right after the man in Mexico was healed. John had to deal with his church, his board and his denomination, though he did not know that yet.

"John, my only concern is that this doesn't destroy your ministry here. The people who come to your church have expectations, as does your board. If those expectations aren't met, there's going to be trouble. If I come to work here I have to know what I'm getting into. Can you see that?"

John completely understood what Edward was saying, and that was the problem. Edward was looking for a place to work that was predictable; a place with established programs, structures and procedures that would allow him to accomplish what John was hiring him to do. John had not thought about what might happen at the church in the immediate future because he wasn't sure of what was going to happen in the immediate present. He had a question for Edward.

"Wouldn't you rather be at a church where God was working, even though it might be messy? Isn't God big enough to help us figure out how to deal with this, instead of trying to figure out how to manage it? Shouldn't we be willing to jump off a cliff and make fools of ourselves to see God do big things?"

It was a persuasive argument, and John delivered it with passion. There was a part of Edward that wanted to throw caution to the wind and sign on the dotted line. Another part of him knew there was trouble on the horizon, trouble he suspected John knew was out there as well. Edward had no doubt he could find another position, but as he sat looking at John he knew this would be a once in a lifetime opportunity, however things turned out. Finally he said,

"In for a penny, in for a pound."

11

Tuesday 7-9 pm

At the end of the meeting there was nothing left to say so they sat in the conference room in silence. They knew what the meeting was going to be about, but they didn't know what was going to happen. Each person came with a slightly different perspective and each was at a different place in their spiritual journey. They shared a common faith and subscribed to the same doctrinal statement. None of them, however, had thought through all the issues they were going to talk about that night.

Most meetings began with the usual small talk; sports, weather, family, jobs and issues involving church members. As each man arrived they remained unusually quiet, waiting for John, who was the last to arrive. He nodded to them as he sat down at the large table and then began talking.

"I know you all have questions about the service on Sunday. Before we get to that, I would like to remind us how we got here. I've been keeping a prayer journal for years, mainly as an aid to remember to pray for certain people. It never occurred to me to keep it to see how God answered my prayers. Lately I have looked at it differently. One day I turned the pages and all they said to me was that God wasn't answering most of my prayers. Unless you consider "no" or "not yet" an answer. While this was happening you know Jerry became ill. I started trying to help Robin cope with what we thought was going to be the loss of her husband to cancer."

He paused for a moment as he thought how he wanted to say what happened next.

"I went to the hospital to visit Jerry, but because his parents were there I decided to go to the chapel and pray. I had prayed many times for Jerry to be healed. This time, as I sat in the chapel, when I was finished, I knew God was going to heal him. I can't explain how I knew, I just knew. I didn't know when, I didn't know what it was going to look like, and I certainly didn't know what the aftermath was going to be. But I knew he was going to be healed. Though I knew this, I still had moments of doubt. When Robin called me Thursday night, I did think he had died, but I guess no one's faith is perfect. I know you want to talk about what happened Sunday, and what the future might look like. I thought it was important to remember how we got here. God answered a prayer and here we are."

If John thought his reminder to the board was going to set a certain tone or change anyone's opinion, he was wrong. The men listened politely, and then the questioning began. Wayne asked John what happened after the service when John prayed for those who remained behind.

"I spent about two hours praying for each of those in the auditorium. Most of them were first time visitors who heard about Jerry's healing. Most wanted me to pray for some kind of physical healing, but not all. Some had needs that involved other people. Some had financial needs. Others wouldn't tell me what their need was; they just wanted me to pray for them. There were at least four people who left that morning healed from what was troubling them. That's about it."

John did not tell them about the woman who asked him to pray that she would get pregnant. He did not know what to make of his brief time with her; he just knew that she was already pregnant. Since it didn't fit into the healing paradigm they were talking about, he let it go. He didn't want to add another dimension to their discussion. Wayne followed up by asking,

"What about Jerry? I didn't see him at church Sunday. When was the last time you talked to him?"

"I haven't talked to Jerry since he left the hospital. I have tried, but I think that he's ducking me. The one real conversation I had with him on Friday wasn't very productive. He doesn't seem to care how he lost the cancer, he's just glad it's gone."

As John was talking, Tim was shaking his head, not believing what he was hearing. Then he said,

"I find it amazing that a man who is healed from cancer can't acknowledge that God was the one who did it."

John shared some of Tim's attitude, but had more time to think about it and offered his perspective.

"I think the more time passes the less likely it is that Jerry is going to attribute his healing to God. Robin knows the truth, but she may not want to continually remind him of what God did for fear of driving him away. It reminds me of the ten lepers who were healed. They all knew it was Jesus who healed them, but only one came back. Jerry was already reluctant to attend church; can you imagine what it would be like for him to show up now with everyone knowing what happened to him?"

Wayne responded,

"We can still be thankful God healed him. We don't know what's going to happen in the future with Jerry, but we do know that God did a great thing in his life. Other people know that too. Look how many new people came to church Sunday."

Wayne was generally upbeat and optimistic in his outlook on life. His words reflected that outlook as well as the fact he didn't see any downside to what happened Sunday. He saw God at work and lots of new people. What was wrong with any of that? It would turn out that at least two board members had some serious concerns. Tim would be the first to ask John what the future was going to hold for the church. John knew the question would come up and had thought how to answer it.

"Tim, let's look at some things that are somewhat out of our control. First, God healed Jerry and set all this in motion. Then, word got out at the hospital about what happened, which is how the newspaper got the story. It turned out Jerry's doctor is married to the news reporter that I talked to Friday, so she had the story from the beginning. My guess is she was going to get it on the news no matter what. Then we have people show up at church because they heard what happened. So far everything is the result of what God did, not anything that we planned."

Tim listened with growing frustration as John talked. He did not need to be reminded of the past, he wanted to know what was going to happen next Sunday, and said so when John finished speaking. John understood Tim was uncomfortable not knowing what the future held, but since John didn't exactly know what the future was going to look like, he took a different approach.

"What do you think we should do Tim? This is new territory for me, just as it is for you."

"Well for one thing, I don't want to see us become a church that focuses on healing. That's not something I'm comfortable with."

"Tim, were you comfortable with God healing Jerry?"

Tim narrowed his eyes, knowing John was leading him into a trap. John didn't think of it that way, but was hoping to help Tim see the inconsistency of his position.

"Of course, we all are. But that was outside the church. If you want to pray for people to be healed in the hospital, that's great."

"You just want it kept out of the church?"

"If healing becomes the main focus of the church, people are going to leave. We both know that."

In Tim's world, people leaving the church was about the worst thing that could happen. When people left they took their wallets with them and offerings went down. When offerings went down, church boards become nervous about how to pay the bills. Michael was sitting across from Tim, nodding his head in agreement as Tim spoke. Before John could respond Michael said,

"I'm also afraid this is going to become about you. You've already been on the news and are being talked about as the pastor who beat cancer."

John heard that once before, and was regretting more than ever his ill-fated decision to let the news reporter interview him. There were two objections he had to deal with, and he chose to speak to the first one.

"I hate to be so blunt, but this church has always been about me. People come because they like how I speak and hopefully they stay because they feel part of a community. From just a human point of view, I've been the face of the church since it started. Let me ask you guys a question. If people were streaming in here to hear me speak, and we had a crowd like we did last Sunday, would you object?"

There was silence in the room because they all knew the answer. They would be thrilled if what John described occurred. They would be talking about how to accommodate all the people instead of how to deal with those who might be coming for a completely different reason. John continued,

"As for what the main focus of the church is going to be, that hasn't changed. We've always been about helping people find God, and then growing in their faith. If God wants to broaden that focus, I'm going to let him decide that."

"What does that mean?" asked Michael.

"I think it means if people keep coming for healing, and Gods continues to heal them, that's what we're going to do. I don't think it means healing will become the main focus of the church. We'll continue to run our normal service and my teaching will be the same as always. However, if people continue to come for healing, I don't know how we can't acknowledge them."

"What if the healings stop? What then?"

"Michael, I can't provide an answer for every conceivable situation. Since it was God who began all this, I would say we trust him for wisdom in how to proceed."

"Are there any other churches in our denomination that focus on healings? What's the denomination's position on healings and miracles?"

Michael knew full well what the denomination's position was on healings and miracles. He had been on the board of the denomination for several years and knew they frowned on other denominations and churches that believed in healing. He was trying to isolate John, but it was not going to work.

"The only position here is God answering prayer. If we don't want God to answer our prayers for people to be healed, then we should stop praying. Michael, is that what you think we should do?"

Michael wanted to say yes, but he knew he couldn't. He didn't mind seeing people healed, he just wanted it done out of sight so it would not affect the church. Then he had a thought.

"Why can't we do this during the week instead of Sunday? If people really want to be healed it would seem to me they would come at another time."

"Michael, I've thought about that. I'm reminded of what Paul said to King Agrippa, that the things concerning Jesus were not done in a corner. I think it's important to let our church know that God is working in our midst and not try to keep it out of the way and manage what he's doing. Does that make sense?"

Of course it made sense, but it was not what Michael wanted to hear. He looked over to Tim to see if he had anything to offer. Tim merely shook his head as if to say, I got nothing. John looked around the group and knew the board was of two minds on what he was proposing. The board generally could reach a consensus on where John wanted to take the church and what he wanted to do. He also knew Tim and Michael were never going to be comfortable with John praying for people to be healed right after the Sunday morning service. As long as Wayne and Randy supported him, there really wasn't anything they could do. They were entering new territory as a board, and it would remain to be seen if they could continue to work together. John did not want their meeting to end on a down note, so he said,

"If you had told me a month ago we would be talking about how God healed a man who had terminal cancer, and that healing would bring the largest amount of visitors to the church we've ever had, I would have said, No way, never going to happen. I know this may make you uncomfortable, but that's okay. I'm uncomfortable too. We need to pray that we'll have the wisdom to respond to what God is doing and let him work, even if it's out of our comfort zone."

Randy was quiet during the meeting, listening to the conversation and keeping his thoughts to himself. He had great respect for John and knew him as well as anyone in the church. He would support John in whatever he wanted to do, but could sense that John was fatigued. He stayed in his seat until the others left, and then said,

"How are you doing? You look really tired."

"It's been a long day, that's for sure. This is the third meeting today where I've had to talk about what God is doing here. Everyone wants to talk about what happened, but nobody really wants to talk about what God did. Does that make any sense?"

Randy was primarily concerned about what was happening to John, so he didn't bother answering John's question.

"You didn't answer my question. How are you holding up? Is there anything I can do to help?"

"Randy, I keep using the phrase "catch-up". I seem to have become the center of everything. I've tried to direct people to God, but I don't seem to be doing a very good job. It's discouraging to say the least. I expected there would be some difficulty with Tim and Michael, but I'm still saddened they don't see what I see."

They were both quiet after John finished speaking. There wasn't really anything left to say that was going to change the situation. John thanked Randy for his concern and asked him to pray that he would be sensitive to God's leading in the coming days. John thought that his day was over and he could head home and get some sleep.

However, he still had one more conversation that evening, one that he was totally unprepared for.

12

Tuesday 10 pm

As he drove home John thought about how different his life had become in the last five days. For ten years he had been pastor of a church that functioned within certain boundaries. He would occasionally change those boundaries to keep the church fresh and relevant. In those ten years he always knew where he was going and what he thought the church would look like. Now he had no idea where he was headed or how the church might change in the coming months. He did not share the apprehension that Tim and Michael expressed, but still doubts came to him when his mind was still.

It was almost 10 when he pulled into the driveway. The lights in the living room were on, something that on a weeknight he would not have expected. John thought Sharon would be asleep by the time he returned home. He got out of the car and walked to the front door, which opened before he could turn the knob. Sharon was standing in the entry and it was evident she had been crying. John closed the door behind him and asked,

"What's wrong?"

He guided Sharon to a chair and sat across from her on the couch. Sharon had a handkerchief in her hand and used it to wipe her eyes before she spoke.

"You know about my mom, don't you?"

"I just found out today. Your dad came to my office today and told me."

John left out Mr. Banks plea for John to pray for his wife to be healed. He didn't know what Sharon knew and didn't want to muddy the waters if it wasn't necessary. Sharon straightened up in the chair and looked John square in the face.

"He says you won't pray for her to be healed. Is that right?"

The last reserves of energy he had were suddenly gone, and John slumped back against the couch. It did not surprise him that Mr. Banks called his daughter and was trying to use her to get to him. He was desperate to do something for his wife, and in his mind John was the last option available. John thought about the irony of Mr. Banks trying to manipulate him into praying for his wife to be healed and what God might think about that. John also knew Mr. Banks wasn't thinking clearly. He was being driven by the one reality in his life; that his wife was going to die.

"Sharon, what happens if I pray for your mother and she dies? What are you and your dad going to think?"

"She's going to die if you don't do something. You prayed for Jerry and he was healed. You prayed for people last Sunday and some of them were healed. How do you know that if you pray for my mom she won't be healed? Why would you pray for people you don't even know and not my mother?"

How was he going to explain to Sharon he had no sense that God wanted him to pray for her mother? He was tempted to take the easy way out and visit her mother tomorrow to pray for her. But he knew it would be a futile gesture, and he did not want to give hope when there wasn't any.

"Sharon, why don't you pray for your mom to be healed? This isn't about me. I don't have any special access to God to heal anyone. Your prayers are just as effective as mine. This is about what God wants to do, not what any person can do."

"But God listens to you, he doesn't listen to me."

"What are you talking about?"

"I told you, he won't answer my prayers."

"How do you know that?"

"Do you see any children in this house?"

The thought that Sharon had been praying for children after her admission about how she might be a bad parent was confusing to say the least. Why pray for children if you thought you would be a terrible parent?

"Sharon, I've prayed for children, too. It would seem God hasn't answered my prayer either."

"But I prayed for something I really didn't want. I'm a hypocrite and God knows it. Why would he answer the prayer of a hypocrite?"

Sharon began crying again and John was quiet as he thought how to respond. He wanted to ask her why she would pray for children if she really didn't want them, but he already knew the answer. She prayed for children because John wanted them. Sharon lived for years with the guilt of praying for something she really didn't want, and the fear that her prayer might be answered. How she managed to maintain any form of emotional stability all those years he couldn't imagine. It was time to get everything in the open, no matter the consequences.

"You prayed for children because I wanted them, right?"

She nodded her head as she wiped the tears from her eyes.

"But you were afraid that if we had kids you wouldn't make a good mother?"

Sharon did not respond to John's question, but then he already knew the answer. He was going to ask the question, and wondered if she would respond.

"Sharon, why on earth do you think you wouldn't be a good mother? Where does this come from?"

She did not respond to his query, but sat quietly in the chair looking at the floor. John did not want to tell her the reason he thought she did not want children, but he was prepared to if she remained silent. Before he had a chance to speak to that issue, she said,

"Are you going to pray for my mother or not?"

He would look back later and think that he was really tired, and that he did not want to talk anymore about why he felt he shouldn't pray for her mother. He was more concerned about how her father had beaten her down when she was a kid. How he left her with a distorted view of God. So he gave in, but not without getting her to answer his question.

"Okay, I'll go over to see your mom tomorrow. But I want you to tell me why you think you would be a bad mother."

There was a flash of hope across her face, and then she took a deep breath and said,

"Because I'm just like my father."

John had no idea how to answer her. If he knew what to say he was too tired to get into a conversation that explored the depths of his wife's life. With an effort he got up from the couch, took her hand and said,

"That's enough for one night. Let's get some sleep."

John did not sleep well that night. Despite the weariness he felt his mind would not shut down. He knew he made a mistake by saying he would visit Sharon's mother and offering hope when he didn't feel there was any. When he finally fell asleep he dreamed he was running along a railway track with a train chasing him. Though he tried to get off the tracks, his legs would only propel him forward. He kept looking over his shoulder as the train got closer. The train never caught up to him, though it was clearly going faster than he was running. When he awoke in the morning it was nearly 9 and Sharon was long gone to work. He quickly got out of bed, went to the bathroom and turned on the shower. Though he slept for over 8 hours, he was not rested and hoped he had enough strength to get through what was going to be a long day.

13

John finally connected with Robin Tuesday afternoon and she agreed to meet with him Wednesday morning. Since it was going to be a warm day he suggested they meet at a Starbucks close to the church so they could sit in the sun. Robin was already at a table when John arrived, sipping her drink and looking over a newspaper. He went to get his coffee and as he waited he looked out the window at Robin sitting in the morning sunshine. It looked like she didn't have a care in the world, reading the newspaper and drinking her coffee. And why should she? Her world had been put back together while John's was falling apart. John took his coffee out the door and walked to Robin's table. He approached her from behind and lightly touched her shoulder in greeting. Then he sat down.

"John, how are you? I don't have a lot of time but I'm so glad to see you."

John was not going to tell her about what happened to him in the last week or any of his troubles. He didn't even know what he wanted to say to her, he just knew they needed to talk.

"It's been quite a week, that's for sure. Why don't you tell me what's happening with your family? How are the girls doing?"

It seemed to John that he was talking to a new person. The last few weeks Jerry was in the hospital had been hard on her. She was not sleeping and she had to take care of her children. She was spending as much time at the hospital as she could, trying to stay positive for

Jerry yet knowing that without a miracle he was going to die. The miracle happened, and it transformed her. She was relaxed, she was smiling and she was seemingly without a care in the world.

"They're so happy to have their daddy back. Jerry isn't going back to work until next week so they're getting to spend a lot of time together. I feel like I'm still playing catch-up to everything that's happened."

"That's the same word I use when I tell people what these last few days have been like. Catch-up."

"I imagine you've been pretty busy. I saw your interview on the news last Friday. And the article in the paper."

"The interview wasn't exactly my finest hour. I kept trying to get God in the conversation and she kept asking questions about me. I guess I was somewhat naïve about how the news media works."

"Well, you're a big part of the story. I've told everyone that you were the only one who believed God would heal Jerry. I know you don't want any credit or anything, but you can't change what happened. I heard what happened at church Sunday. It seems that God isn't done using you, is he?"

"No, not yet."

He wanted to add that some people would be happy if God stopped using him, but thought the better of it. He knew Robin would have to leave soon and he wanted to talk about Jerry. John asked her if Jerry had said anything that would indicate his heart might be softening toward God.

"He said he would like to come to church this Sunday. He thought it would be too soon this past Sunday. He didn't want to be the center of attention. I think he knows people are going to look at him differently, but he's okay with that. I think he's had some time to think about what's happened to him and he might be ready to talk with you."

Finally, John thought, he would get a chance to talk with Jerry about what God had done in his life. He was also glad to hear Jerry was willing to come to church, something he had seldom done in the past. John knew there were two parts to his prayer, the healing was answered but Jerry was still on the outside of faith looking in. Though it appeared he was getting closer.

"Let him know that any time he would like to talk, I'm available. Is there anything I can do for you? Any way the church can help right now?"

"Well, we need a babysitter for Saturday night. We're going out on a date for the first time in months. The girl I usually use is not available."

"I think Sharon and I could manage that. Let me call her and I'll get back to you."

After Robin left John spent some time finishing his coffee and enjoying the sunshine. He had a lunch meeting with the regional director of the denomination who had called Tuesday. The man didn't say why he wanted to meet; only that it was important. John wanted to savor the conversation with Robin; so far it was the highpoint of his week. If they watched Robin's girls Saturday night he would get a chance to talk with Jerry and maybe set up a time to meet with him next week. Things were looking up.

14

Wednesday 12 pm

They met at a restaurant near the church. John did not know the man but knew of his position in the denomination. The seminary that John attended was part of a denomination and when John graduated the regional director approached him about planting a church. The denomination promised to pay John's salary and all start-up expenses for the first three years of the new church's existence. Because starting a new church was more appealing to John than pastoring a more traditional one, he agreed. The man he was having lunch with was the current regional director for the denomination. Although the man did not give a reason why he wanted to meet, John could guess.

His name was Lyle and he was about the age of John's father. They spent the first few minutes getting acquainted and looking over the menu. After they ordered Lyle quickly changed the topic of conversation.

"I was at your church last Sunday. Quite a service."

John had no idea where Lyle wanted to go with him but was willing to listen to what he had to say. He did not, however, want to spend any more time than necessary getting to the point.

"You must have seen something in the media about the man in our church who was healed."

"Not exactly."

"I assume you weren't there by chance?"

"No. I got a call from one of your members. He's a friend of mine. He thought I should be there. He wanted an outside opinion."

Though Lyle used the word "member", John understood that he meant board member. He doubted anyone in the church would have a reason to call the regional director of the denomination. Most of those who attended did not even realize the church belonged to a denomination. It was just their church.

"You mean one of my board members? And what would he want your opinion about?"

"I think he wanted someone who has some experience in different types of church settings to sort of evaluate what might happen."

"You mean he was afraid that things might get out of control?"

"You saw how many visitors came to your church because one man was healed. That's not normal for any church. Some churches wouldn't know how to handle a situation like that."

"I don't know how to handle a situation like that. I knew there would be people who were going to be there because they heard something miraculous had occurred. I wasn't going to turn people away because they heard God did something big."

"I understand that you were in a tough spot. I don't know that I would have done anything different."

Lyle wanted to say more but John interrupted him.

"I don't consider it a tough spot when God answers a prayer and heals someone who was almost dead. I get that's not normal and out of our experience as a denomination, but I'm not going to dictate to God how he can or can't work in my church."

"Praying for someone to be healed is one thing. We all want that. It's another to turn a church into a place where people come to be healed. You have to think of how you want people to view your church."

John did not want to get into an argument. He knew why Lyle wanted to meet with him and what he wanted to accomplish. Lyle wanted the church to return to normal, put God back in the box and get on with its business. John responded,

"I'm not sure at all that we want God to heal people. We pray for that, but I doubt we actually want it to happen all the time. Our expectations of how God will answer prayer have been so low that when he does do something that astounds us, we thank him and hope that he doesn't do it again so we're not considered fanatics."

John spoke slowly, calmly and without emotion. Lyle would not know it, but John's words were the result of his years praying and waiting. Lyle could see John had thought about what was happening in his church and would probably not be dissuaded by anything he was going to say. He still had two cards left to play, so he threw the first one on the table.

"You know, it's not the position of our denomination to focus on healings and miracles in our churches. I know you're aware of that. It also isn't the position of the seminary you graduated from."

"Lyle, I don't have a position on any of this. I prayed for a man to be healed and he was. I'm playing catch-up to everything that's happening. I don't know what this is going to look like for the church. However, I believe God is big enough to handle whatever happens. I think we're a little past denominational positions, don't you?"

"I've seen this happen in other churches. It never ends well. Churches split; people walk away from the faith. You have to think about your place in the denomination."

"I didn't know I had a place in the denomination. The only time I ever see anyone from the denomination is when I go to the annual pastor's conference. What are you talking about?"

It was time to throw the second card on the table, though Lyle by now realized John would not be easily swayed.

"The denomination paid for your church, at least for the first three years. We paid your salary and all of your church's expenses. We did that because we thought you were a good investment. Someone who represented our beliefs and values. You're not going to turn your back on those who were there for you at the beginning, are you?"

Like nearly every other area of life, this was coming down to money. John had been around long enough to know that nearly everything in churches revolved around money. It didn't necessarily bother him; it was just a fact of his existence as a pastor. Churches, denominations, seminaries, regional directors and pastors all needed money to survive. In this case, though, he refused to let the fact that the church years ago had been funded by the denomination enter into his part of the conversation.

"What do I do about these people who are going to come because they want somebody to pray for them?"

"You mean they're coming because they want you to heal them. Let's not forget that. You become the reason people come to church."

"I'm already the reason people come to the church. We both know that. I was the reason people came before any of this. People come because they can relate to what I say and the vision and tone I set for the church. And you didn't answer my question."

"If you go back to what you did before, and remove the emphasis on healing and miracles, your church will go back to normal."

John wanted to scream that he didn't want the church to go back to normal, but instead said,

"What if God keeps healing people in answer to our prayers? What do I do then?"

Sometimes people say things they don't mean. They just get caught up in the moment. Sometimes people say things that they mean, though it may sound incredulous to the person who hears it. John would never know why Lyle said what he did, but it wouldn't matter. Their paths would never cross again. With a completely straight face Lyle said,

"Stop praying for them to be healed."

15

Wednesday 2 pm

It took John about 30 minutes to drive to Mr. Bank's house. John left the restaurant before his food arrived, tossing down some money as he left without speaking. He wanted to give Lyle the benefit of the doubt, but it was hard. Lyle's commitment to his denomination's doctrinal position was more important to him than stepping outside of it for a moment to watch God work. John could understand the man's motives. Lyle was afraid that if John continued down the path he was on, the denomination would sooner or later have to come in and clean up the resulting mess. John thought it odd that he seemed to be the only one to understand that when God did big things it was bound to be messy. Nearly every revival and movement John could think of in church history had its promoters and detractors within the church. There were those who understood this and those who retreated into the world of wanting God to work in normal, predictable and manageable ways. Lyle appeared to be firmly in the last group.

John arrived at the Bank's residence and parked on the street, waiting a few moments before heading for the door. Mr. Banks was watching from the living room and opened the door before he could knock. John nodded at him in greeting and sat down on the living room couch. Mrs. Banks was not in the room; presumably she was upstairs in her bedroom. Mr. Banks sat down opposite John, not meeting his gaze. It struck John that while Robin exuded life and happiness, Mr. Banks was where Robin was just a week ago. He looked exhausted, there was no color in his face and he was constantly wringing his hands. When the silence finally became uncomfortable, at least to John, he said,

"How is your wife today?"

"She doesn't complain, but it's becoming harder for her to breath. The doctor is going to put her on oxygen tomorrow."

Mr. Banks was still not looking at John, who decided there was no point in making small talk. He got up from the couch and said,

"Let me go talk with her."

Mr. Banks rose at the same time, intending to go with John upstairs. John stopped and gently said,

"It would be better if you stayed here. I'd like to talk to her alone. I think she'll be more receptive that way."

Mr. Banks was used to getting his way, especially in his own house. He hesitated for a moment, and for the first time looked John in the face. John had seen that look before, but then Mr. Banks sat back down in defeat. He looked out the window to show his displeasure, which John had already felt from the look on his face. John turned away and went up the stairs toward the bedroom. The door was closed and he knocked lightly, and then he opened it and entered.

She was lying in the bed propped up with pillows. She wasn't reading or watching TV; she was just lying there with her eyes closed. It didn't seem to John that she was in pain, but she was having trouble breathing. John stood at the door for a moment, and then closed it behind him. There was a chair by head of the bed; he turned it around so he could face her when he spoke. He now understood Mr. Banks desperation. She was ghostly in appearance with a drawn face and nearly translucent skin.

He thought back to when he was sitting in the chapel praying for Jerry to be healed. How he knew God would answer that prayer. John would never be able to explain to anyone how he knew that prayer was going to be answered. In the same way, he would not be able to explain to Sharon or Mr. Banks why he knew there was no point in praying for Mrs. Banks to be healed. It was just something he knew in his heart. While he was thinking he felt Mrs. Banks hand touching his arm. Her eyes opened and she said,

"I heard that you were coming to see me."

"Yes. It's been a long time."

"I'm sorry about that. It wasn't what I wanted."

They had only spoken a few words to each other and the specter of Mr. Banks was already hovering over them. The thought that Mr. Banks could exercise such control over her and deny her the opportunity to see her daughter and son-in-law for extended periods of time brought tears to John's eyes. He turned his head from her view and wiped them on his sleeve and said,

"Well, let's not worry about the past. Are you in any pain? Is there anything that I can do for you?"

"I don't have any pain; it's just hard for me to breath. I can't do the things that need to be done around the house. I don't know how Harold is managing. He doesn't do well when things aren't done in a certain order. He thinks he needs to be in charge of everything."

She said those words with a smile, but he knew the truth. He thought about Mr. Banks sitting downstairs. How he must feel not being able to be in control of the conversation. The thought brought him no joy. It just made John feel sorry for the years Mrs. Banks had to live under the same roof with him. Then he thought about Sharon and her brother living for years with Mr. Banks and never being able to meet his expectations. Like many other things in life, it just didn't seem fair.

"Mrs. Banks, when was the last time you talked with Sharon? Has she been to see you lately?"

"I think that Harold talked with her yesterday. At least that's what he told me. I don't remember the last time I talked with her. How is she?"

"She's fine. I know that she misses you and would like to come see you. Would that be alright?"

Mrs. Banks did not immediately respond, but turned her head and looked away. She was still touching his arm and he could feel her grip get tighter.

"I would like to see her. But you will have to ask Harold."

"I can't imagine that he would have a problem with her coming to visit. I'll bring her tomorrow after she gets off work."

"I know you're doing what you think is right, but I would appreciate it if you asked him anyway. I'm the one who has to live with him, you know."

John was sure Mrs. Banks knew she was dying. Yet she couldn't bring herself to do something without getting her husband's permission. What the repercussions would be if he brought Sharon over to visit her mother without getting his permission he couldn't imagine, but he didn't want to give Mrs. Banks any additional stress.

"I'll ask him when I leave."

Before he could say anything more, Mr. Banks, who had quietly entered the room while they were talking, said,

"You'll ask me what?"

They both turned their heads in surprise at the sound of his voice. Mr. Banks again asked,

"You'll ask me what?"

"I'm going to bring Sharon over tomorrow after she gets off work to see her mother. I was going to let you know on my way out."

John looked to see how Mr. Banks would react to being told that something was going to happen rather than asking his permission. Before he could react, Mrs. Banks said,

"I would like to see her Harold. I don't think that's an unreasonable request considering the fact that I'm dying."

Mr. Banks was quick to respond.

"Who told you that you were dying? No one has said that."

"I'm sick, but I'm not stupid. I can feel that I'm dying. My heart has been going out for years. We both know that. You just won't face it, that's all."

John guessed this was probably the most straightforward Mrs. Banks had been with her husband in many years. Even though she was dying and had nothing left to lose by telling him what she felt, he knew it must have been hard to break out of a pattern she had been in most of her life.

Mr. Banks looked at John and without saying anything John knew what he was thinking. Mr. Banks wanted to know if John had already prayed for his wife to be healed. If so, John thought he would probably ask him to leave. Then it struck John, as Mr. Banks stood in the doorway, that he probably wanted his wife healed so he wouldn't lose the one person he still had some control over. His kids were long gone, he was retired from the ministry and if he lost his wife he would not only be alone, he would be a man without anyone to bully. It was a dark motive to attribute to someone, but John knew it was true. He also thought how unfair it was that this kind, decent woman had to live with Mr. Banks for almost 45 years.

"Mr. Banks, could you leave us alone for a few minutes?"

Mr. Banks understood from John's words that he had yet to pray for his wife. He was torn between wanting to know what was going to happen and wanting John to fulfill his promise to him.

"Well, don't be too long. She needs to rest."

He waited until the door was shut, and then he turned to Mrs. Banks. She watched as Mr. Banks left the room and then she closed her eyes and breathed a little easier. Though he thought he knew what God wanted for her, he asked,

"Mrs. Banks, would you like me to pray for you to be healed?"

"Why on earth would I want that?"

There was real surprise on her face when she spoke, and her voice was firm and clear. He smiled at her and then took her hand. He prayed she would have comfort, he prayed she would find relief from any pain she was feeling and she would find her happiness in her relationship with God. When he was done, he told her he would bring Sharon by the next day.

"Thank you. Can you do one more thing for me?"

"Of course."

"You have to let it go. There's nothing you can do and it will only make it harder for you and Sharon."

"I'll try, but it won't be easy. But I guess you know that."

He bent over her and kissed her on the cheek, and then he was gone. When he got to the living room Mr. Banks rose from his chair and was about to speak, but as he looked at John he hesitated. John stopped at the end of the stairs and was waiting for Mr. Banks to ask him the question.

"You didn't, did you?"

"No. I didn't. She told me she didn't want to be healed. It's her life, so I respected her wishes."

For the second time in a week, Mr. Banks did not get what he wanted. John watched him as he absorbed the news that his wife was surely going to die. John expected that he might take a parting shot, but instead Mr. Banks said, in a whisper,

"She'd rather die than live with me."

16

John arrived at the hospital just as it was getting light. Robert's surgery was scheduled for 8.30 and John wanted to spend some time with him before they took him to the operating room. He was sitting by Robert's bed talking with him about his experience with Mr. and Mrs. Banks the day before. Robert listened as John recounted how he thought Mr. Banks wanted his wife healed so he would still have someone to control. Robert wasn't so sure.

"I have met men like him before. He may actually love his wife but for reasons that he may not even be aware of, he's unable to show it. You shouldn't be too hard on him. He's lived for years knowing that he's a lousy husband and father. Believe me, he thinks less of himself than you do, that's for sure."

"Even if that's true, it doesn't mean he couldn't have learned to treat his family decently. I still think he's a bully. I doubt he'll ever be anything else."

Robert thought about this for a moment, then said,

"Have you talked to him about how you think he treats his wife and kids?"

"No, but in the last two weeks I've been with him twice and it hasn't been in the least bit pleasant. I can't imagine what he'd be like if I told him what I think about the number he has done on his kids, let alone his wife."

"And you're going to see him tonight with Sharon?"

"Yeah. Sharon hasn't seen her mom in months. There's no telling how much longer her mom is going to live."

"I can understand why she didn't want you to pray for her to be healed. She's ready to go, but my guess is that he's scared to death of dying."

"Why would you think that? He's so full of himself he might think that heaven was made just for him."

John spoke with some bitterness and Robert knew John was still on edge from his time with Mr. Banks. Robert was older and more experienced than John and knew Mr. Banks probably lived in fear of having to explain himself to God.

"That generation of pastors, especially in his denomination, have always believed that though you don't earn your way to heaven, you can earn points with God by keeping the rules as best you can. There's only one problem. He can't keep the rules, whatever they might be, and he knows it. So he just keeps trying harder and as he keeps failing he gets more miserable. Then guess who gets the brunt of his misery? I've been down that road myself. It wasn't easy to get off."

"How did you get off?"

"It's a long story. I'll tell it to you someday."

As he spoke, a nurse came in to give Robert a sedative. He winced as she gave him the shot and then he said,

"You think about what I said. When you see him tonight, you ask him this one thing. Why does he think God is angry with him? See what he says. It might surprise you."

John rose from his chair as an orderly came into the room with a gurney. With some help from the orderly, Robert slid onto the gurney for his ride to the operating room. The surgery would take a few hours, and Robert would be in recovery for several after that. John thought about leaving and coming back in the morning, but decided to stay until the surgery was over. He followed as the orderly wheeled Robert down the hallway toward the operating rooms. When John could go no further he said,

"I'll see you tomorrow morning."

Robert nodded in acknowledgment then closed his eyes as the sedative took effect. John turned and walked down to the waiting room. There was only one other person in the room, a young woman holding a baby who looked about a year old. John sat down across from her and smiled as their eyes met. The baby was holding a rattle and shaking it back and forth. It slipped from the baby's hand and landed on the floor next to John. He picked it up and handed it to the mother. She thanked John, and he said to her,

"I'm waiting on a friend who is having heart bypass surgery. It's routine surgery, but I wanted to be here for him since his kids couldn't make it. We're both pastors, he's been a mentor to me most of my career. How old is your son?"

"He's almost one. He wants to get down and play but he'll just crawl away. It's easier to just hold him. He'll get tired eventually and want to sleep."

"I am going to be here awhile. If you need some help with your son, I'd be glad to play with him."

"No, that's okay. I'm used to doing this. This hospital is our second home."

"You have a family member here?"

"My older son is having surgery today. For a tumor on his kidney. It's really rare and the doctors aren't sure what's going to happen. They won't give me a straight answer."

John knew from his own experience with doctors, and from spending a lot of time visiting patients and family in hospitals, that when doctors were vague it meant they were hedging their bets and did not want to offer hope if there wasn't any. As he thought about how he might respond, he got the feeling he should pray for her son. Then he understood, in the same way he understood about Jerry, if he prayed for this woman's son he would be healed.

No, he thought to himself. He could not do that again. He was not prepared to have God intervene miraculously in someone's life and start another roller coaster he would have to ride. He didn't even know this woman. Why would God want to heal her son and not his friend who was going to have his chest cut open in just a few minutes? He was just about to leave and head over to the cafeteria when she said to him,

"Could you watch him for a moment while I use the restroom?"

"Sure. What's his name?"

"This one is Sean. My other son is Robbie. He's the one having the surgery. My name is Megan."

John took Sean from his mother and began to bounce him on his knee. He talked to the little boy while he waited for the mother to return. To John's surprise the little boy did not cry when his mother left.

"Sean, I know you don't understand any of this, but I want you to know your brother is going to be okay. I want you to know that God is going to take away the tumor that's on his kidney. I want you to remember in the years to come when you're playing with your brother it's because God was merciful to you and your mom. I don't understand any of this either little guy, I just want you to know that today God is going to do something big."

He was still speaking to the little boy when his mother returned. She reached down for the child and he said to her,

"My name is John. Would it be alright if I prayed for Robbie?"

She sat down across from him, holding her child and looking straight at John. She slowly nodded her head and John prayed for Robbie. He prayed Robbie would be brave, that the doctors would be wise in how they treated him, that God would comfort Megan and finally, that God would do something big in the lives of this family he had just met. When he finished he said to Megan,

"I'm going to go over to the cafeteria and get something to eat. Can I bring you back something? Some coffee? Something for Sean?"

"Coffee would be nice. Just black."

She paused a moment, then said,

"Thank you for praying for my son."

"Of course, no problem. I'll be back in just a bit."

When John prayed for Jerry to be healed, he was not being prepped for surgery. John didn't know when God was going to heal Jerry; he just knew it was going to happen. Here, the timeline was now. If God was going to heal Robbie it would be that morning. He did not understand what God was doing with him and didn't think he could handle another outcome similar to what occurred with Jerry. It was one thing to pray for people who came to his church on Sunday, it was quite another to pray for a child he had never met in a hospital he just happened to be in that day. It was not lost on him he had prayed for God to do something big, but it was unsettling to him the way it was all unfolding.

He spent about 30 minutes in the cafeteria drinking a cup of coffee and eating some pastry. As he sat at a table he kept thinking that though he didn't understand what was happening, God did, and that should be enough. After getting a cup of coffee for Megan, John set off for the waiting room. It was a short walk through a few corridors and then one floor on the elevator. When he came out of the elevator he saw Megan standing and talking with two doctors. They were dressed in green surgical gowns and one of them had two x-rays in his hand. He held one up to the light and put his finger on the film, shaking his head as he spoke. Then he held the other one up and again put his finger on the film. John was about thirty feet away and could not hear the conversation, but he knew what the doctor was saying. He could read the body language of the doctor who was explaining to Megan that the last x-ray they took prior to surgery did not show any tumor. One showed it there, and one showed it gone.

John stepped back against the wall to think about what he should do. He did not want to speak with any doctors present, so he would wait until they left. Then he thought maybe the best thing to do was just leave and let this unfold without him. After what happened with Jerry he did not want to be any part of the story and figured that God could take care of the events that would surround the healing. He pushed the button for the elevator and waited, hoping to escape without being seen by the mother. As the elevator arrived he turned for one last look. The mother turned and saw him. Their eyes briefly met, John smiled at her, and then he was gone.

17

Thursday 5 pm

John met Sharon at her office and together they drove to her
parent's home. He had not told her that on his previous visit he
did not pray for her mother to be healed. He knew he had to tell
her before they arrived, but he was not looking forward to the
conversation. After driving for ten minutes he knew he had to get it
out in the open.

"I told you when I saw your mom the other day that I prayed for
her. But I didn't tell you she didn't want me to pray for her to be
healed. I was prepared to, but she was adamant. I thought you should
know before you saw her."

Sharon looked straight ahead, absorbing what she had been told.
When she responded, John was not prepared for what she said.

"That doesn't surprise me. It's the one way she could get back at
him."

Though the thought had occurred to John, he said to her,

"I don't understand."

"The one thing he can't tell her to do is to not die. He can
control everything else, but he can't control that. I still can't believe
he asked you to do something for him. I don't think he has ever done
anything like that before."

"You mean do something for your mom?"

"No, I mean do something for him. This is about him, not my
mother."

John had never heard Sharon speak about her father like that. He couldn't ever remember a time when she talked about him in a personal way. It was always, my father did this, and my father did that, and usually related to his role as a pastor. He asked her another question, hoping she would continue to talk about him as she was doing.

"Why do you think he's making this about him?"

But she was done talking. She knew she needed to talk with someone about her father, but it was not going to be John. At least not yet. He knew the conversation was over when she said,

"If you had lived with him, you would know."

As they continued the drive to her parent's home, Sharon took out her cell phone. She ran her finger down the contacts screen until she found who she was looking for. Turning the phone so John could not see who she was contacting, she sent a text asking the contact a specific question. She held the phone in her hand as she waited for a reply. When it vibrated, she looked at the message on the screen and then typed in reply, Thanks. See you then.

The sun was setting as they pulled up to the Bank's home. They walked up to the front door and again Mr. Banks opened it before they could knock. Sharon entered first and before anyone else could speak, she said to her father,

"Is she upstairs?"

He nodded in reply and Sharon turned and walked up the stairs. John watched as Mr. Banks thought about following her, and then said,

"Why don't we sit down in the living room and let them have some time together."

Mr. Banks put up no resistance and sat down on the couch. John sat across from him and noticed that Mr. Banks appearance had again changed for the worst. He was weary, looked like he had not slept and was wearing the same clothes. John didn't know how much time they would have alone, so he did not wait to begin the conversation.

"How is your wife doing today? Did they put her on oxygen?"

"Yes. It seems to help. But it's not going to solve anything."

"What do you mean by that Mr. Banks?"

"I mean she's going to die. And there is nothing that anyone can do about it."

"Mr. Banks, we're all going to die. Even people God heals are going to die. You know this. You know your wife is going to heaven. I know that you will miss her, but you're acting like someone who has no hope."

"I'm not talking about hope. I'm not talking about heaven. I'm talking about when she's gone I won't have anyone. I'll be completely alone."

John wanted to add "With no one left to control or boss around", but he didn't. He thought about what Robert had told him about Mr. Banks. That the man might not know the reasons why he treated his family the way he did, or why he felt he needed that control. John was not without compassion, but he was coming to understand how the man had wrecked the lives of his wife and children.

"Mr. Banks, most people at the end of their lives end up living alone. As Christians we should be different. We may live alone, but God is always with us. Don't you agree?"

John wanted to bring God into the conversation so he could possibly explore what Robert thought was Mr. Banks perceived notion that God was angry with him. As they spoke, Mr. Banks kept looking toward the stairs, wondering what was transpiring between his wife and daughter. He either didn't hear the question John asked or was ignoring him because he did not respond.

"Mr. Banks?"

Brought out of his reverie, Mr. Banks said,

"What? What do you want?"

John needed to bring Mr. Banks back to the conversation and try and get inside the man's head.

"You told me once that God is displeased with you. And that he wouldn't answer your prayers. Why do you think that?"

Mr. Banks was never going to reveal to John his inner thoughts or motives or why he thought God might be angry with him. He spent a lifetime living according to a set of rules that brought him no peace or assurance. He tried to force those rules on his family and had only succeeded in driving away his children and reducing his wife to a compliant servant. It finally dawned on him what he had done, but he was powerless to change, even if he wanted to. The slight opening of his heart John had seen was an aberration, and it would not happen again.

"I never said God was displeased with me. You must have misunderstood. Your generation is so presumptuous. You hear what you want to hear and base everything on your feelings. The only thing I have ever asked from you, you denied me. I don't think we really have anything to talk about."

John was an unusually patient person. He seldom lost his temper; he thought before he spoke and tried to be considerate of other people's feelings. He was a good listener and generally felt compassion for people, something others sensed in him. He now knew that he was at a dead end with Mr. Banks and for the first time in memory he did not hold back anything when he replied.

"If I was God, I would be displeased with you. You're a miserable old man who doesn't understand grace, compassion or how much God loves people. You live in fear of God and you should, because you're going to have to give an account of how badly you treated your family all these years. I'm only beginning to understand how your treatment of Sharon has robbed her of having any real joy in life. She could never meet your ridiculous standards and has felt like a failure her whole life. She's tried to make up for it by being the best person she could, and like you she is always in her own mind coming up short. You just don't realize that God knows you can't meet his expectations because he doesn't have any. He just wants you, not the things you think you need to do to please him. There might be hope for Sharon, I doubt if there's any for you."

No one had ever spoken to Mr. Banks in such a manner. John did not raise his voice, but there was an intensity to match what he was saying. Despite having little sleep for many days, Mr. Banks found the energy to say to John,

"Get out. Now."

"Mr. Banks, that may have worked on your wife and kids and maybe people in your church. But that doesn't work with me. You don't have any hold on me, you can't mess my life up, and I'm not leaving until Sharon is done talking with her mother."

Mr. Banks rose from the couch and was going to go up the stairs, presumably to put an end to Sharon meeting with her mother. He was no doubt thinking that would be the quickest way to get John out of his house. John knew what he was intending and said,

"Mr. Banks, I'm a lot younger and a whole lot stronger than you. I'm not going to let you interrupt them. So please, sit back down."

Mr. Banks was torn, but he knew from the tone of John's voice that he meant what he said. Though he kept a reign on his emotions, inside he was seething and wanted in some way to strike out at John. Nothing came to his mind, however, and he understood he was beaten. But he didn't have to like it.

"You'll regret someday what you just said to me."

"No I won't. I should have said it a long time ago. But as you know we can't change the past, as much as we might like to."

The next twenty minutes were among the most surreal of John's life. The two men sat across from each other and did not say a word. John sat on the couch and after a few minutes took out his phone and began to check his emails. He was not uncomfortable just sitting there and would wait all evening if Sharon needed the time. He could not imagine what Mr. Banks was thinking. He was just sitting on the couch staring into space, no doubt waiting for the evening to end. John thought about the young mother he had met at the hospital and tried to picture in his mind how her day progressed. He thought he remembered her wearing a wedding ring. Did she call her husband and tell him that their son's tumor was gone? What would have been his reaction? What would the doctors tell her? "We can't find the tumor, we don't know why, but we aren't going to do the surgery and we haven't seen anything like this before." Would she tell them that he had prayed for her son? Would God come into the conversation?

It was while he was thinking about his morning at the hospital he heard Sharon coming down the stairs. She had been with her mother for about an hour, and when she stepped into the living room she looked first at her father sitting on the couch. She didn't say anything to him and John could not tell what she was thinking. She broke the tension that was beginning to develop in the room by saying to John,

"Let's go."

John was off the couch in a second and opened the front door, holding it open so Sharon could go out first. Instead she said to him,

"You go out, I'll be right behind you."

John did as he was told and wondered what Sharon was going to say to her father. She said things to John that evening that were completely out of character for her, and he hoped that she would be that honest with her father. He sat in the car for a few moments, and then watched as Sharon came out the front door, closing it behind her. When she was seated he started the car and pulled away from the curb. John wanted to say something so he started with what he thought might be safe.

"How was your mom?"

"She didn't talk that much because she had the oxygen mask on. I don't think we really had a lot to say to each other. Neither one of us knows how to be a daughter or mother and you can't fix a relationship when someone is going to die soon."

John was again taken aback by how much Sharon was revealing about her life and feelings. What brought her to this place he had no idea. He hoped this signaled a new and deeper place in their marriage. He decided to ask her one more question.

"What did you say to your father?"

"I told him if he needed any help taking care of my mother to call me. I don't think that will happen, but I wanted to make the offer."

"Why don't you think he would want your help?"

"Because I also told him I'm not going to let him control my life like he did my mother's. That I'm going to get out from under his shadow if it's the last thing I ever do."

There wasn't anything John wanted to add so he remained silent as they drove home. He thought about the two events that he was part of that day. Though he had been part of healing a young boy that he might never meet, he really believed the bigger miracle was Sharon taking some tentative steps out of her former way of life. When they arrived home and were getting out of the car she said to him,

"It's been a long day, but I'm not that tired. What about you?"

18

Friday 8 am

Robert's surgery had gone well. When John arrived at the hospital Friday morning he was still in intensive care but was alert and eating what passed for breakfast. John sat at his bedside and told him what transpired the night before. He told Robert how Sharon was revealing things about her life he had never heard before. He asked Robert why that might be happening now.

"My guess is this is all related to God healing Jerry. For some reason God has jumped into your life in a big way. You said you've been praying that God would do something big. Looks like your prayer has been answered."

"I need to tell you something else. Something that happened yesterday."

John then recounted for Robert his encounter with the young mother in the waiting room and how he was moved to pray for her son. How when he returned he was sure the son had been healed. How he felt it was best that he leave and let God take care of the situation.

"Why did you leave when you saw what was happening with the doctors? It seems that you could have provided some context for her."

"Hey, I wasn't going to get in another conversation with doctors about God doing something miraculous. I really didn't think it through. I just saw the doctors there and left."

"I suspect some of this has to do with what happened to Jerry?"

"Maybe. I got worked pretty good and I didn't want that to happen again. On the other hand, there is some movement with Jerry. We're watching their kids tomorrow night and Robin tells me that he's coming to church Sunday. He wants to talk with me about what's happened to him."

Robert finished his food while John was talking and pushed the tray back from his bed. There was something he thought John was missing in everything that was happening to him. He thought for a moment, then said,

"I know you're trying your best to stay in the background, but that's just not going to be possible. Let me ask you a question. In the Book of Acts did the apostles who did miracles try and stay in the background? Would they have left that young mother alone in a waiting room? Would they have felt insecure being around doctors because the doctors might act superior with them? Wouldn't they have risked being misunderstood and ridiculed as long as they could point to Jesus as the one who was healing people?"

John had known Robert a long time and appreciated his insight and counsel. He knew what Robert was saying, that he was too worried about what people were going to think of him and the criticism he might get in the process. As much as John wanted God to get the credit for what was happening, he equally wanted to remain unscathed personally. In his mind his motives were clear, but he also knew few people did anything with completely pure motives. He also remembered how he told Edward they ought to walk toward the messes instead of away from them.

"Don't let this go to your head, but you might be right. I guess if God is big enough to heal people he's big enough to take care of whatever mess I might get myself into."

"There's something else. I don't think this is going to last forever. I think God drops into our lives to do special things, and then after a while events return to what we might call "normal". You might want to keep that in mind when you're dealing with your board. They're going to think this is what your church will look like forever when in all likelihood this is going to peak sometime. That's what happens in every revival or movement, but you know that."

John had not thought about anything ending. He had just experienced God healing another person the day before. He knew Robert was right, and part of him wanted things to return to normal. He also knew he might never have the chance to see God do miraculous things in his ministry again. When John didn't immediately respond, Robert said,

"What are you going to do about Sharon?"

"I'm not going to do anything. She's said things in the last two days about her life she has never shared with me before. I'm going to let her find her way through all of this. If she wants to talk with me about it, that's fine. But I'm not going to force anything."

Just then a nurse came into the room to check on Robert and remove his breakfast tray. She looked at the various monitors measuring Robert's vital signs and asked him how he was feeling. Before she could leave Robert asked her if anything unusual had happened yesterday in the hospital. She stopped and said,

"Why do you ask?"

"My friend here is a pastor. He prayed with a young mother whose son was having surgery yesterday. We were just wondering how the surgery went. He had a tumor on his kidney."

She looked at John for a moment, and then pulled the door shut so she could talk freely.

"He's right down the hall recovering. The doctors are now saying there wasn't any tumor. The surgeon is blaming the radiologist and the radiologist is blaming the kid's oncologist. When they cut him open there was nothing. Everything was normal. He'll probably leave in a couple days. The mom is down there if you want to talk to her."

John looked at Robert who was smiling at what he had set in motion. John said to the nurse,

"Sure. Could you walk me down there?"

He followed her out of Robert's room and past the nurse's station. John only had a few moments to think about what he was going to say. When he came to the room he could see through the glass walls the mother sitting by the bed. The boy was looking up at the television and the mother was gazing down at her phone. The nurse knocked on the glass and opened the door. She stood aside as John walked in and stood at the foot of the bed. The mother looked up and then recognized John.

"I was just down the hall visiting my friend who had surgery yesterday. The nurse mentioned that you were here. I thought I might look in and see how you're doing."

She put her phone on the bed and said,

"It turns out there wasn't any tumor. His surgeon can't explain it, but when they went to take it out it wasn't there. Somebody made a mistake and somebody is going to pay. I'm looking for a lawyer who will take the case. You just can't do unnecessary surgery on a kid and get away with it."

No thank you for coming, no my kid is going to live, no recognition of John having played a part in her son's life and certainly no recognition of God. John knew he was probably not going to convince her God healed her son, but he wanted her to know the truth.

"I'm glad your son is going to be fine. I don't think the doctors made any mistake. I think God removed the tumor and healed your son. I wanted you to know that."

"Why would God do that? I'm not sure I even believe in God."

"I believe God sometimes breaks into our lives and does miraculous things to draw our attention to him. That's what I think happened in this case."

She thought for a moment, looked at her son, and said,

"But I remember your prayer. You didn't pray for Robbie to be healed. You prayed that he would be brave and something about the doctors. I don't remember hearing the word "heal"."

He was in a box of his own making and he could not get out. Why hadn't he prayed for the boy to be healed? It wasn't any lack of faith; he knew exactly what was going to happen. Robert was right.

He just wanted God to work and not have to answer any questions, explain how he knew, draw attention to himself, or get involved in any more drama. He wasn't ready to give up yet, and tried one more time to bring God into the conversation.

"I did pray that God would do something big. Nothing is much bigger than removing a tumor."

"But the doctors are saying the tumor may not have even been there."

She stood up and took John's arm, opened the door and went out into the hallway. She lowered her voice and said,

"I've got a good thing here. These doctors blew it. They did surgery on a kid who wasn't even sick. They made a big mistake. And they're going to pay."

John thought she was done talking, but he was wrong.

"I really need the money. If God had anything to do with this, that's great. I just don't care."

John reached into his wallet and took out his business card. He gave it to her and said if there was anything he could ever do for her to call. She took it without comment and went back into her son's room. Just like that it was over. He stood outside the room and looked around at nurses going about their business; patients being taken in and out of their rooms, visitors coming and going, and doctors looking at charts before going in to see their patients. God had invaded this place, he thought, and done something marvelous. And no one knew.

He walked slowly back to Robert's room, shut the door, and then stood at the foot of the bed. Robert could read the look on John's face but wanted to know exactly what happened. John merely said,

"You can't serve God and money."

Robert thought for a moment, pulled himself up in the bed, and said,

"She wants to sue somebody."

John nodded in response, and then shared his thought that God had done something miraculous and nobody knew about it. He wanted to say, What's the point? but thought the better of it.

"This story isn't completely written yet. You don't know how this is going to turn out. You and I know what happened."

There was a knock on the door and John turned to see a doctor looking through the glass wall. Robert motioned for him to enter.

"Excuse me; can I talk to the pastor for a minute?"

John looked at the doctor, and then said,

"How do you know I'm a pastor? Have we met before?"

Robert was in a hospital that was an hour from John's home, one that John seldom visited.

"No, but I know who you are. Can we talk?"

He held the door indicating he would like John to follow him, but John said,

"We can talk here. Robert is a retired pastor and my friend."

The doctor looked uncomfortable, but shut the door to have some privacy. He had a folder in his hands, opened it and took out two x-rays. Both John and Robert immediately knew what was happening.

"I saw you yesterday morning in the waiting room. I didn't put it together until I saw you talking to her in the boy's room. You prayed for the kid to be healed, didn't you? Just like the man who had cancer. I recognize you from the TV."

"I did, yes."

The doctor held one of the x-rays up to the light and pointed to a dark spot on the film.

"This x-ray was taken two days ago. We want to know the exact location of the tumor before we operate. If it's gotten any bigger. If it's bleeding, things like that. That's a tumor, no doubt about it. It's rare in a kid this young. When I opened him up yesterday, there was no tumor. It was gone. It just wasn't there. This is the x-ray we took after we closed him up."

John had never looked at an x-ray before, but he could tell the difference between the two. On the second x-ray, taken after the aborted operation, there was no dark mass.

"What do you want from me?"

"I want to know how this happened."

"I prayed for her son to be healed and God listened. That's about it."

"It can't be that simple or you would be going from room to room in this hospital praying for people to be healed. Am I right?"

"Doctor, I can't explain how or why God choses to heal the people he does. It may sound silly to you, but I just do what he tells me."

The doctor again put the two x-rays up to the light, looking from one to the other. After satisfying himself that something miraculous had happened, he said to John,

"Let me buy you a cup of coffee."

After talking with John for about half an hour in the cafeteria, he had to excuse himself. He wanted to talk with John further, and made an appointment to see him later that week. The doctor would come to believe in God, and would be instrumental in leading others to him in the coming years.

19

Amy was mildly surprised when she received Sharon's text the night before. She thought Sharon was done with counseling, at least for the time being. Amy had no idea why Sharon would want to see her unless it had something to do with John. Amy knew about Jerry, and wondered about how they both were dealing with the aftermath. Because her husband had been a pastor, Amy knew there was certain to be consequences, both good and bad, from something miraculous happening in John's ministry. Like every other session they had together, Sharon arrived right at noon. When she was settled in the chair across from Amy's desk she said,

"I'd like to talk about my father."

Amy noticed Sharon was more relaxed than she'd been in the past. She wasn't surprised that Sharon jumped right into the conversation, getting right to the point was part of her character.

"Okay. But I would like to know why now. I've wanted to talk about this before but you weren't willing."

"My mother's dying. I said some things to him last night I still can't believe came out of my mouth. I don't think the relationship will ever be the same."

She thought for a moment, then added,

"If there ever was a relationship."

"I'm sorry about your mother. What did you tell him?"

"I told him I wasn't going to let him control my life anymore. That I was going to get

out from under his shadow."

There was so much in Sharon's words Amy almost didn't know where to begin. Amy suspected Sharon's father had cast a long shadow over her, but never had the freedom to explore the relationship. Now it was being handed to her on a silver platter.

"How do you think he's been controlling your life? You've been out of the house for a

lot of years."

The answers were not going to come easily. Sharon was going to think back over her life

and find words to describe what she experienced growing up under her father's roof. She

thought for a moment, and then said,

"I never missed a church service. I never missed a midweek prayer meeting. I never

missed youth group. I was never late for dinner. I always did my homework and usually got A's on my report card. I didn't know it at the time, but I think I did all those things for him."

"Lots of kids want to please their parents. Why do you think this was a bad thing?"

"Because the only time he ever acknowledged us was when we met his expectations. And

then it was only to say that we did what we were supposed to do. It was harder for my brother. I

usually did what he wanted. My brother was more inclined to go his own way. And he paid for it."

"How?"

"He was beaten. And I don't mean spanked. I mean beaten. I had to watch, and it scared me into doing what he wanted."

"What did your mother think about that?"

"I think she knew how to survive living with him. You have to remember, she comes

from a generation of Christian women who usually didn't work and were taught the husband is the undisputed leader of the home. She tried to get my brother to do what my father said to make his life easier, but I think he thought the only way he was going to get any attention from his father was to disobey. How's that for being messed up?"

"I'm guessing your brother doesn't communicate much with your dad?"

"He doesn't talk to anyone in the family. I think he's been trying to put all of that behind him."

As Sharon talked more about her past and different experiences that illustrated how her father held her at arm's length, Amy realized Sharon probably viewed God in the same way she viewed her father. Demanding, distant and with expectations that Sharon could never meet. Their time was running out and she wanted to get the idea that Sharon might have a distorted view of God into their discussion.

"Sharon, what would happen if you stopped going to church? Let's say you took a break for a while, just to get a different perspective on life."

Amy didn't expect Sharon would say that God would be mad at her. Amy had to start somewhere, and thought that a question about being obedient would help Sharon see how she viewed her relationship to God.

"Why would I stop going to church? What would that solve?"

"I don't know that it would solve anything. But what do you think your life would look like?"

Sharon had been with Amy long enough to know what she was trying to do. The only reason Amy would ask a question like that was to get Sharon to think about something she didn't want to ask directly. She had more than once short circuited Amy by telling her to just ask

what she wanted without trying to finesse her. She did so again.

"What do you really want to know?"

"Okay, I'll ask you straight out. What do you have to do to make God mad?"

Sharon had not expected that. She didn't know what she was expecting, but no one had ever asked her before if she thought God was mad at her. The answer was obvious.

"Nothing."

"What do you mean nothing?"

"I mean that I don't have to do anything to make God mad. I think he's always mad."

Sharon spoke the words calmly, and with an assurance Amy found breathtaking. Amy suspected that was how Sharon viewed God, but was still surprised at how easily the words came from her.

"Why would God be mad at you? Aren't you his beloved child?"

"Of course. But I also know that God hates sin. Even though I'm his child I still sin. I think he takes sin seriously, don't you. When I sin, it displeases him. Maybe mad is too strong a word, but I know he's not happy."

Where to start, Amy thought. Sharon spent a lifetime trying to meet the expectations of her father, and had never succeeded. Like many people, she looked at God in the same manner, as someone she needed to please through her obedience. Though she probably understood it on some level, Sharon knew she could never be obedient enough to make God completely happy. What she was missing was the idea that God had no expectations of her, and her sin did not affect her relationship with him in the way she thought.

"I hate to end without exploring this in more depth, but I have another appointment. Can we meet again next week? I know there are other things we might want to talk about."

They had not talked about John. They had not talked about her mother. They had not talked about what was happening at the church. And they had not talked about children. If Sharon realized how her father had affected her life she might think differently about having children. But it would have to wait.

"Yes, I would like that."

Amy had never heard Sharon say that she would look forward to their next meeting. After two years Sharon was finally at the point where Amy felt she could help her. Amy could not know it, but her next meeting would not be with Sharon, but with John. And it would be a matter of life and death.

20

Friday 2 pm

John needed to spend Friday afternoon finishing his sermon for Sunday. After leaving the hospital, he drove straight to his office. He returned some phone calls worked through lunch finishing what he wanted to say. He was going to deviate from the series of messages on relationships and talk about how God answers prayer. After last Sunday's service he wanted to provide some Biblical context so people could understand what was happening in the church. He told Sharon he might have to stay late at the office because he only had that afternoon and evening to finish his message. His board wanted to meet before the Sunday service and the only time he could fit them in was Saturday morning. They were watching Robin and Jerry's kids Saturday night so he was pressed for time. John was interrupted just then by Susan knocking on his door. She opened it and said,

"Edward is here to see you. Shall I send him in?"

John was going to introduce Edward to the church Sunday morning. They had not talked since Tuesday and though John really didn't have the time, he told Susan to send him in.

When he sat down across from John's desk Edward asked,

"How is your friend doing? The one who had surgery yesterday."

"He seems to be doing well. I saw him this morning and he thinks the doctor will let him go home Monday or Tuesday."

John thought about telling Edward about the young boy at the hospital. Since it didn't directly affect what was happening at the church, he decided against it.

"Have you settled in yet? Is there anything you need for your office? If there is just let Susan know and she'll fix you up."

Edward nodded in response.

"Thanks. I will. I just wanted to see how you're doing. I can guess that you've had a busy week. I know that pastors sometimes don't have anyone to talk to about what's going on."

Edward was right, most pastors did not have anyone they could talk with about personal issues or the difficulties they might be having in their churches. John was somewhat unique because he met with Robert nearly every week. He appreciated that Edward was trying to look after him and said,

"I know what you mean. My friend in the hospital is a retired pastor. We usually meet every week and we're pretty candid with each other about what's going on in our lives."

There was silence as the two men sat across from each other. John waited to see if Edward was done, and then broke the silence by asking,

"Is there anything else you wanted to talk about?"

"I wanted to know if you're going to pray for people after the service this Sunday."

John knew if there were people who came for that reason he would do exactly what he had done the week before. He felt God was still willing to work through him, though he knew Robert was correct in thinking this kind of ministry would not last forever.

"I think so. If God is willing to work I don't see I have any choice. What are you thinking?"

"I'd like to join you, if that's all right."

"In for a penny, in for a pound?"

"Something like that."

"You understand that my board isn't completely unanimous about all this. A couple of the guys really want things to go back to the way it used to be. Part of me wants things to go back as well. I know I spoke about not being afraid to be involved when things get messy, but I want you to know I'm way out on a limb here. I can't see where any of this is going, but I guess that's not necessarily a bad thing. If I could see the future I might get cold feet."

Edward knew if they could see the future they might try and manipulate the present to get the future they wanted. He asked John what kind of future he would like to see for the church. Before all of this happened, John knew what kind of church he wanted. He wanted a church that was welcoming, that didn't exclude anyone because of either what they believed or how they looked. A church that taught Biblical truth without a hard edge and could truly be called a community. He also wanted a church that helped people become more like Jesus, and to that end he hired Edward. John understood that real life change usually occurred when people were in relationship with others who shared the same values and beliefs. If Edward could help get people into groups where they could experience that kind of relationship, John would feel that the church was moving closer to what he envisioned.

The question before them was, What happens when God breaks into your plans in a startling and miraculous way? John understood the fears of Michael and Tim, who thought the church was going to be unalterably changed by the events surrounding Jerry's healing. There really wasn't anything he could do but ride the whirlwind. He wasn't about to hinder what God was doing, even if he could.

"So you don't have a problem with me helping you Sunday?"

"We're assuming that we'll have the same type of group that we had last Sunday. If we do, then let's see how God leads and be ready to jump in."

John paused while he thought about what he was agreeing to. It had not entered his mind that anyone else in the church would be interested in praying for people to be healed. Certainly none of his board members offered to become involved. John didn't want to ask Edward about his motives or reasons. He knew God wasn't limited to using any one person to accomplish his purposes. He even thought getting Edward involved might take some of the spotlight off him, which he had been trying to do since it all began.

"Anything else? I need to finish up my message this afternoon. I'm really busy tomorrow."

"Nope. I'll be here Sunday and we'll see what God does."

Edward would not see John on Sunday, but on Monday. And it would be under circumstances that neither of them could foresee.

21

Saturday 8 am

John had resisted meeting with the board, saying they had a scheduled meeting the next week. But Tim and Michael pushed to meet Saturday, wanting an update on what was going to happen on Sunday. Wayne and Randy agreed to meet on the condition they keep the meeting as short as possible. They met in the conference room off the auditorium and engaged in small talk until John arrived.

"Sorry I'm a little late. I know some of you have other things on your schedule so why don't we get going."

He prayed God would give them wisdom on how to best serve him in the coming days, and help them be sensitive to what God wanted to do in the church. When he finished, he began by giving them a brief update on Robin and Jerry.

"I wanted you to know Sharon and I are babysitting tonight so Robin and Jerry can have some time for themselves. When I talked to Robin this week, she told me Jerry plans on coming to church tomorrow and would like to talk with me sometime soon. This is really good news. I am going to try and set up a time to meet with him when I see them tonight."

The men all nodded in agreement, but that wasn't why they were meeting. John had just finished speaking when Tim brought them right to what he thought the meeting needed to be about.

"What are we doing about the service tomorrow? What's your plan? I'd like to have an idea what's going to happen."

John understood Tim was also speaking for Michael. They had both been blindsided by what happened the week before and did not want that experience repeated. What they wanted was a normal service. John wasn't prepared to give them the assurance they were looking for.

"Guys, you know how I feel about this. If we get a lot of people showing up like we did last week, I'm going to ask them to stay if they want prayer. I don't see how I can do anything else. Several of the people I prayed with last week left healed. If God is going to work, I think we should let him. That's my opinion. Tim, what do you think we should do tomorrow?"

John normally did not ask the board for their opinion on what the church should or should not do. His normal procedure was to tell them what his plans were and ask them what they thought. They seldom had any problem with anything he wanted to do because the church was growing at what they considered an acceptable rate. Tim had thought about what should happen on Sunday, and he was ready for John's question.

"First, I think we should limit the number of people in the auditorium to the number we're permitted by the fire marshal. I also don't think we should ask our people to give up their seats for visitors. We can put those who won't fit into the auditorium in the other rooms like we did last week. They can look at video monitors and enjoy the service that way."

Tim wasn't done speaking but John interrupted him at that point.

"Don't you think it sets a bad example when we don't put our visitors first? Remember Jesus' teaching about taking the last seat at the feast? One of our main goals is to get more visitors to come to our church. Let's put them first."

"But our members are the ones who support the church. If we make it so that they can't be in the service they might stop coming."

"I think you should give our members more credit than that. I would like to treat our visitors the best we can so we don't stand in the way of them hearing the gospel."

"But they're not coming to hear the gospel. They're coming to be healed. What are we saying to people if all we offer them is a chance to get better physically? We devalue the gospel."

There was so much in what Tim said that John did not know where to begin. In the end it all came down to fear. Fear that things would get out of control. Fear that people would leave. Fear that the fire marshal would show up and find they were in violation of the fire code. Fear that the church would become something unrecognizable. John understood fear, but his fears were different. They centered on his ability to do what he felt God called him to do. John decided to deal with one of the issues Tim raised head on.

"What's wrong with people coming to be healed? Did Jesus ever turn away anyone who came to be healed?"

The answer was obvious, and Tim could not think how to reply. John continued,

"I don't think it devalues the gospel to pray for those who come because God is working in a special way to heal and restore people. This moment won't last forever and I suspect things will eventually return to what we had before."

"But you don't know that for sure, do you? That things will return to normal?"

Michael joined the conversation, echoing what Tim was saying.

It did not escape John that Michael and Tim were willing to exchange the power of God displayed in Jerry's life, and then in the lives of others, for a return to what they considered "normal". He did not want to express it that way to them, but he did ask them,

"Would you rather I stop praying for people to be healed, and just run a normal service?"

Michael looked at Tim and then said,

"I think that would be the best course of action. We can still preach the gospel to those who come. Some of them might even get saved."

And then he said something John had heard before.

"I think we also need to consider the denomination. We owe them a lot as a church. We should think about how this looks to them."

Wayne and Randy, who had been observing rather than participating, both looked at John for understanding. Then Randy said to Michael,

"What does the denomination have to do with any of this? I can't remember the last time we even talked about the denomination."

John looked quickly at Michael, and then turned to Randy and said,

"I think Michael is referring to the fact the denomination funded the church for its first three years. Though that was a long time ago. Isn't that what you meant?"

Michael replied by saying,

"Yes, but that's not all. Our denomination doesn't want its churches to focus on things like healing, speaking in tongues and miracles. Our denomination was founded on preaching the Bible and proclaiming the gospel. They might ask us to leave if we continue down this path."

Randy wanted to speak, but John waved his hand at him so he could respond.

"Guys, we're not on any path. This has all happened in the last week. I think we're getting way ahead of ourselves when we talk about being asked to leave the denomination. Let's try and stay in the moment and continue to see how this plays out. I think we should meet every week to discuss what's happening and share our concerns. What do you think?"

Wayne, who had another appointment that morning, was the first to respond.

"Sounds good to me. I hate to be the first to leave, but I've got to coach my son's soccer game."

With those words he was out of his chair and then through the door. The other men knew the meeting was essentially over and also rose from their chairs, but none of them spoke. They had not come to any consensus and knew John was going ahead with his plans to have the same type of service as last Sunday. What they did not know was that the Sunday service would be completely different from what they could imagine, and John would have no part in it at all.

22

Saturday 11.30 am

J ohn spent a few hours after the meeting in his office putting the final touches on his message. When he was done he wandered around the church thinking about the Sunday service. It was over a week removed from the events that brought dozens of visitors to the church. Most of those visitors came because of the coverage Jerry's healing generated in the newspaper and on television. John had no idea who was going to show up Sunday though he hoped some of those who were healed would return out of gratitude for what God did for them. Though his experience with the young mother whose son was healed was fresh in his mind, he believed at least some of the visitors from the week before would be in attendance.

It was to that audience he wanted to speak. He was using as his text the story of Jesus feeding the five thousand. John wanted to emphasize that while Jesus was willing to meet the physical needs of people, having those needs met was not an end in itself. Whether or not God healed someone, whether or not God met a financial need, whether or not God did something that could be considered miraculous in someone's life, the bigger miracle would always be God changing the direction and meaning of a person's life when they believed in Jesus.

John was walking through the lobby when he heard voices coming from inside the auditorium. He walked up to the closed doors and listened to the voices coming from the other side. After a moment he realized it was the three young guys who ran the sound booth on Sundays. The booth was located at the back of the auditorium, between the two doors that allowed entry into the large room. As he listened he found they were checking the connections that took the service into the rooms used the week before to accommodate the large amount of visitors. John was ready to open the door and join the conversation when he heard one of the men say,

"My dad wants us to keep the camera rolling after the service is over. He wants us to tape what happens after the service."

"Why would we do that? We didn't do it last week."

"I don't know. He just asked if we could do it."

"Should we ask John?"

"I don't think we need to do that. It might make him self-conscious if he knew he was being taped healing people."

"How do we know he's going to do the same thing he did last week?"

"What would you do if a bunch of people showed up at your church who wanted you to pray for them? I don't think he has a choice, does he?"

"He's the pastor. He can do whatever he wants."

"It must be cool seeing people healed because you prayed for them."

"Yeah, but I've heard that people who get healed seldom stay healed. It has something to do with how your mind can trick your body into thinking its better."

"Where did you hear that?"

"My dad told me lots of faith healers say they've healed people but then the people just get sick again."

"You think John is a faith healer? That's not him."

"What would you call it when you pray for people to be healed?"

"You make it sound like a bad thing."

"I don't think it's good or bad. I just know my dad says lots of people are talking about this."

"Well he should know. He's on the board."

John slowly walked away from the door and out of the lobby, not wanting to be discovered. He headed back toward his office and went inside; closing the door behind him, though there was little chance of him being disturbed. If things were normal, he would have spent some time chatting with the three guys as they worked. He could hear from their conversation that things at the church were far from normal. As he sat in his chair he again ran through the options open to him for the service tomorrow. First, he could run a repeat of last Sunday and pray for healing for those who came for that reason. Second, he could announce that those who came wanting prayer for healing or other reasons could meet at the church during the week. He guessed that some would make the effort, but he also knew some would see this for what it was, trying to keep the church as "normal" as possible. Finally, he could abandon any thought of healing people and instead preach to the common need of everyone, the need of salvation.

It was tempting to take the path of least resistance. There was also the thought that God would not want the church to become divided. He knew he might be able to use the momentum of God healing Jerry and the others to move the church forward, especially in the area of discipleship. His addition of Edward for just that purpose could be seen as more than a happy coincident. Maybe God had broken through into the life of the church for that reason, to bring a deeper level of commitment to the larger membership.

He also knew he could not function with a divided board. Michael and Tim were good men, but they were never going to be onboard with the direction he was taking the church. Then he was pulled up short. He was not taking the church in any direction. He was merely responding to what God was doing. He had not planned anything. He had no new programs. He hadn't added any new structures. He was just trying to find a place for God to work in the lives of people. There was also the idea Robert shared with him that this was a special time that would not last forever. The problem was he didn't have forever to figure out what he should do. It would turn out he didn't even have tomorrow.

Jerry and Robin showed up right at five thirty, kids in tow. John was waiting on the front porch and noticed the two girls held tightly to their dad's hand as they walked across the lawn. He wondered what the last week was like for them as their lives returned to normal. John hoped in some way they understood God was responsible for their dad coming home from the hospital. John bent over to greet the girls, extending his hand.

"Hi girls. I hope you're ready to have some fun tonight."

The two girls did not immediately respond, but continued to hold Jerry's hands. It was awkward for a moment until Robin said,

"Come on girls, let's go inside and find Sharon."

Sharon was the girls Sunday school teacher, and had known them all their life. John and Jerry watched them disappear into the house, and then Jerry said,

"I sure appreciate you taking the kids for us. This is the first time since I got sick that we've had any time for ourselves."

"I'm glad we could do it. You look great, how are you feeling?"

"I'm still getting my stamina back. I spent too much time lying around in a hospital bed. My muscles got soft. I'm going back to work Monday. I still can't believe it's over."

John wanted to jump in and ask Jerry if he had thought about why he was able to leave the hospital and get back to his family, but Jerry wasn't through talking.

"I know the only reason that I'm here talking to you is because you prayed for me. You know I've never been religious. I thought it was a good thing for Robin and the kids to go to church, but it never interested me. I'm going to come to church tomorrow, but I don't want it to be a big thing. Is that possible?"

"Of course. Why don't you come about five minutes after the service starts? I'll make sure the ushers save you seats in the back. If you want you can leave just before we end. We'll try to make it as anonymous as possible. How does that sound?"

"Thanks. I appreciate that. The girls will be happy I'm going to church. I won't have to come up with any more excuses."

"Maybe we could have lunch this week. I bet you got tired of hospital food."

"That's great. I'll call you when I know my schedule. I'm going to be busy catching up at work."

"Whatever you can work out. Let's go inside and see what the girls are up to."

Jerry and Robin left a few minutes later, first for dinner and then a movie. John could tell Jerry was close, real close. His experience with people was that if they were willing to meet with him and discuss spiritual things, they usually became believers. In Jerry's case, John knew Jerry would never have thought about going to church or meeting with him if he had not been healed. He hoped Jerry would be the first of many who would come to faith as a result of God displaying his power in the church. It would not only bring momentum into the church, but give John some cover with Michael and Tim. John wasn't being crass, he was just being practical. If he wasn't able to change their minds, at least he wanted to have results to show them. They would be thrilled if he came to faith and joined the church. Which now looked like a distinct possibility.

After a dinner of tacos and chips, Sharon was setting up a movie for the kids in the family room. John was cleaning up the kitchen when his phone rang. He pulled it out of his pocket and looked at the number. He didn't recognize it and almost let the call go to voicemail. Instead, he answered, listened for a moment, and then said,

"Right. We're watching the kids while they're out tonight. I think they'll be back around 11."

It was the girl's grandfather, asking if John and Sharon were babysitting. John was distracted for a moment as Sharon called from the family room asking if he was ready for the movie to begin. John was not hearing what the man was saying.

"I'm sorry. I missed that. What did you say?"

He put his hand over his ear so he could hear better, and then listened as the man spoke. After a moment he turned to look at the two girls, who were sitting in front of the television waiting for him. Sharon came into the kitchen and saw the blank expression on John's face. He held his hand up to her so she wouldn't speak, and then he said into the phone,

"Which hospital?"

Part Three

1

Saturday 8 pm

John ended the call and stood in the kitchen suspended in time. He was aware Sharon was standing next to him, waiting for him to say something. He looked back into the family room and saw the two little girls, now orphans, sitting on the floor in front of the television. He had to speak, but could not form words. At that moment it seemed possible he might never move from that spot. If he did his world would fall apart.

"John, what's happened?"

"You need to go and start the movie."

"What? What are you talking about?"

"You need to start the movie."

Sharon understood John wanted her to get the girls distracted. She went back into the family room, started the movie, and then returned to the kitchen. John was still standing next to the kitchen counter, trying to figure out what to do next. He went to the sink and splashed some water on his face, and then sat down at the table. Sharon sat next to him and waited for him to speak. For a moment John didn't say anything. He turned again to look through the doorway at the girls sitting on the floor, their backs leaning against the couch. He then turned to Sharon and said in a low voice,

"Jerry and Robin have been in an accident. They're both dead. That was Jerry's dad. I have to go to the hospital and identify them for the State Police."

"What? What do you mean they're dead? They were just here a couple hours ago."

John was slowly coming back to some sort of reality and thinking about the things he needed to do. He heard Sharon speak, but the words did not register.

"I'm sorry. What did you say?"

"Maybe there's been a mistake."

He wished there had been a mistake. How he wished he had not answered his phone. That maybe this was a dream and he would wake up and find everything was normal. He looked at his phone, which was still in his hand and knew for certain what had happened. John slowly shook his head.

"No. I don't think so. You didn't hear his voice. I have to go to the hospital. Jerry's parents won't get there until early in the morning. I'll need to be there for them."

"What about the girls? What do we tell them?"

"They'll have to spend the night. I guess we'll tell them that mom and dad are going to be out late so they wanted them to spend the night."

"We're going to lie to them? About their parents dying?"

"Don't you think it's best if their grandparents do that? They can't be here until tomorrow morning at the earliest. I'm open to other ideas if you have any."

John got up from the table, went to the refrigerator and got himself a glass of water. For the third time he looked at the girls who were utterly content watching the movie, unaware they had lost their mom and dad. There wasn't any other alternative that came to Sharon's as she sat at the table, so she said,

"I guess you're right. What do you think is going to happen to them?"

"That won't be up to us. I've got to get going. I'll call you when I get there and know something. I probably won't be back until the morning."

"What are you going to do about church?"

That thought had raced across his mind, but he hadn't yet focused on how he was going to cover the service. He knew there would be no way he could be there, but figured something would come to him.

"I'll make some calls on the drive down to the hospital and get it sorted out. I'm sorry to have to leave you here alone. You might want to call someone just to have another person here."

"No, I'll be all right. Maybe we should pray before you leave."

He put down the glass of water and got his keys and wallet from the kitchen table. The day was warm but he still got a light jacket from the hall closet. Before he opened the front door and left for the hospital, he turned to her and said,

"I don't think I can pray right now. Maybe later, but not right now."

She watched him get into his car and pull out into the street. She had never heard him say anything like that before, though he had been through many crises in his role as a pastor. But this was different. Though it had not yet occurred to her, and would not occur to him until later that night, everything in his life revolved around Jerry's healing. Now that Jerry was gone, there was a hole developing in John's spirit that could consume him if left unchecked.

He called Edward first. He told him what happened and asked if he could give a short message. John would have Michael give a brief announcement before the message about the accident, and then Edward would speak to the congregation. He would prefer that Edward spoke on something that would be relevant to the situation, but knew that would be asking a lot. Edward, however, said that would not be a problem. Then he asked John what he should do about those who might be visiting, those who came specifically for healing. He was surprised when John said,

"You really think people will want us to pray for them after the guy who was healed of a brain tumor ends up dead a week later?"

Edward was taken aback by John's words. He paused for a moment, and then said,

"I won't do anything this week, then. I'll just acknowledge those who are visitors and tell them we're glad they came. Is it all right if I ask the church to pray for the family? Especially the girls."

"I'm not sure the family would appreciate us praying for them considering the circumstances. But you do what you want."

He talked to Michael next and kept the call short. Michael asked if Edward was capable of delivering on such short notice and John said,

"We'll see."

It was just after eight and John figured Robert would still be awake. He pulled off the highway so he could find the number for the hospital. When his call was answered, he asked for Robert's room. It rang three times before Robert picked up.

"Hey. It's me. You still up?"

"It's only a little past eight. Why do you ask?"

"I'm heading down to the hospital. I'll be there in about twenty minutes. I have to see someone. Can I come up after that?"

"You have a member of your church here? Is it an emergency?"

"Yeah, it is. I'll see you in an hour or so."

John didn't want to talk anymore on the phone and left Robert hanging. There had been enough time since Jerry's dad called for his emotions to settle. He was still on the edge, but he would be able to function. The one thought he kept forcing himself to dwell on was that he had to keep it together at least until he saw Jerry's parents. They could deal with the girls, but he had to be able to help them when they arrived at the hospital. All the details that happened when people died would need attention. He had experience navigating through hospitals, funeral homes and the police. The presence of a pastor made everything run smoothly. He was the one person people counted on to be calm during death.

When he arrived at the hospital emergency entrance there were three ambulances and several police cars parked in the driveway. He then realized there might be more victims. After parking his car, he walked into the emergency room and went to the admitting desk.

There were at least 20 people in the waiting room, which was not unusual for a Saturday night. He waited for a moment until a receptionist came out through the doors that led into the emergency room itself. She bent down over a desk and was busy putting together paperwork when he got her attention by saying,

"I'm here to identify two bodies."

She looked up at John and said,

"Let me get you a nurse. I'll be right back."

She returned with a nurse moments later who motioned for John to follow her inside the large metal doors. Though it was obviously busy, the emergency room was eerily quiet. The nurse led him past numerous exam rooms then stopped in front of a closed door. There was no window and nothing written on the outside to indicate the purpose of the room he was about to enter.

"Wait here. I need to get the police. It'll just be a minute."

"Okay. Thanks."

John knew that just inside the door were the bodies of Jerry and Robin. He had no idea what to expect or how he might react when he went into the room. John had watched people die before, but their deaths were usually expected and generally peaceful and without a lot of drama. He would comfort the family members, if there were any, and then help them through the myriad details that culminated in a funeral or memorial service.

The nurse returned quickly with a police officer who had been at the scene of the accident. He shook John's hand, and then John asked him about the accident. It was a bad one, the officer said. A pickup truck had run a red light and hit their car on the passenger side, causing it to flip and rollover at least three times. The driver of the pickup survived but was in critical condition. Jerry and Robin died at the scene of multiple injuries. When John explained that the family had asked him to identify the bodies, the police officer said,

"Have you done this before?"

"No."

"The nurse and I will go in with you. She'll raise the sheet on each body and you'll need to look at each one and be certain. Okay?"

John nodded in response, and the nurse opened the door. John followed her inside. The room was bare except for two gurneys placed side by side. He watched as the nurse pulled the sheet back on the first body. He said,

"That's Robin."

Moments later he said,

"That's Jerry."

When he was done, he turned and walked out of the room and waited outside for the nurse and police officer. He was surprised at how matter of fact the experience was for him. It would occur to him, in view of what happened later, that he wasn't ready to let his grief surface just yet. After the nurse closed the door he said to her,

"My guess is his parents will want to see them when they get here tomorrow morning. Is that possible?"

"They'll be in the hospital morgue until a funeral home comes for them. It shouldn't be a problem. Do you want us to call a funeral home? We do that sometimes when the family is from out of town."

"I'll call them and let you know what they want to do."

He gave both the nurse and the police officer his business card and then went outside to call Jerry's parents. They were still at home when he called, deciding on what exactly they needed to bring with them. He confirmed to them it was Jerry and Robin, and told them what the police officer said about the accident. John said how sorry he was and asked if he should contact a funeral home for them. Jerry's father explained he had already talked to a funeral home and was making arrangements to bring the bodies back to their town for burial. John told him the girls were spending the night with them and did not yet know about the accident. He thought it would be best if the grandparents broke the news to them that their parents had died in an accident. There was a pause in the conversation, and then Jerry's father said,

"I think it would be best if you did that. We don't know our grandchildren very well. It would probably be easier coming from you."

Jerry's parents had their son later in life and must have been in their mid-70's, John thought. When Robin and John were meeting regularly, she seldom spoke about them. John wondered what kind of relationship existed between the two families.

"Okay, Sharon and I will do it in the morning. I guess I'll see you in about eight hours."

When there was no response John looked at his phone and saw that the call had ended. It was time to go see Robert.

2

Saturday 9.30 pm

Robert had been moved out of intensive care and was in a different wing of the hospital. It took John several minutes to walk through the corridors and find the right elevator. He stepped out of the elevator into another waiting area and looked to see which way he needed to go to find Robert's room. There was a sign on the wall indicating that Robert's room was down the hallway to the left. He turned to go and then thought how seeing Robert was going to help with anything. Jerry and Robin would still be dead. The girls would still be orphans. The biggest problem he was going to face was just beginning to force its way into his consciousness. It wasn't something he had to do; it was something he had to understand. Robert had been his friend and mentor for many years, and helped him through any number of difficult situations. But nothing like this.

Robert was sitting up in bed watching television. John came into the room and sat down in a chair that was at the head of the bed. Robert turned off the television and waited for John to say something. John said nothing; he just sat there with a blank look on his face, staring straight ahead. It was the first time all day he didn't have to do anything, and his mind was content to coast in neutral. It had been a little over an hour since he talked to Jerry's father. John didn't know what he was feeling or thinking. He was just sitting there in Robert's hospital room waiting for something to happen.

It was the ringing of his phone that broke the silence. John reached into his pocket, looked at the number and tossed the phone to Robert, who caught it awkwardly. He could see it was Sharon, so he pressed the answer button.

"Hi Sharon, it's Robert. John is here with me but he's not able to come to the phone right now. Can you tell me what's happened?"

Robert listened while Sharon related what she knew about the events of the night. She wanted to know if John had identified the bodies, that it was actually Jerry and Robin.

"He just got to my room when he had to step out, so I don't know. He should be right back. I'll have him call you when he returns."

Robert put the phone down on the bed and searched for the right words to say. He understood now why John was just sitting there.

"Thanks for covering for me. It's been a long day. I just needed to sit for a minute and not have to think about anything."

Robert picked up the phone and held it out toward John.

"Do you want to call her back?"

John slowly shook his head and did not reach for the phone Robert held out to him. Just then a nurse walked by and saw John through the glass wall of Robert's room. She stopped, came into the doorway, and said,

"I'm sorry. Visiting hours are over."

"He's a pastor. He's got some people here and just stopped by to see me. We're old friends."

"Okay, just don't stay too long. You need your rest."

John followed her with his eyes as she turned and left, and then said,

"To tell you the truth, I don't know why I'm here. I should be heading home to get some sleep. I have to meet Jerry's parents here early in the morning."

"I doubt you're going to sleep much tonight no matter where you are."

Silence crept into the room again when John did not respond. Robert knew John was either going to talk or he wasn't. There wasn't any point in pushing him. They sat there for the next hour, each with their own thoughts. When Robert had to get up to use the restroom John's eyes did not follow him nor did he seem to notice. The spell was broken when John's phone began ringing again. Robert picked it up and was going to answer it when John said,

"You better let me answer. It'll be Sharon."

Robert held the phone out for John who reached from the chair and took it from his hand. He didn't bother to say "hello", he just started talking.

"Sorry I didn't call you sooner. They're here, probably in the hospital morgue by now. I spoke to Jerry's dad and he wants us to talk to the girls. They should be here around 5, so I'm just going to stay here. I don't see the point in coming home just to turn around and come back. It seems pointless". He wanted to add that everything seemed pointless at the moment, but thought the better of it.

John listened for a moment, and then ended the call. Robert could not tell if they were done talking or if John had simply said enough and hung up on Sharon. Robert tried to imagine what thoughts were going through John's mind. Just a week ago John was dealing with the repercussions of God breaking into his world by healing Jerry. That event brought about circumstances John could not have foreseen, including the reaction from his board when he prayed for people in his church, the unwanted news coverage, the initial refusal of Jerry to attribute his healing to God and the incident at the hospital just two days ago when the young boy was healed.

Robert did not know everything that John was dealing with in his life. His encounters with Mr. Banks in the last few days. How Sharon was just beginning to open up about her relationship with her father and how it had affected her all her life. John's continuing uncertainty about what his future ministry was going to look like. The bottom had fallen out of his life, and there was only one person who could catch him. If John would allow him. If not, John's fall could leave him questioning everything he ever believed. John was still just sitting in the chair, holding his phone, and Robert now thought he did not have anything to lose by trying to begin a conversation.

"It might help if I knew what you're thinking."

John's concentration was broken when Robert spoke. He hadn't been doing anything but sitting in the chair trying to keep thoughts from forming.

"Help what?"

"You just lost two people that were a big part of your life. You had to identify their bodies for the police. You have to tell their children that mom and dad are dead. This is going to be your life for a while. I think it would be good to talk about what you're feeling."

John stood up and turned to look out the glass wall of Robert's room. It was getting late and there was little movement on the floor so John was basically staring off into space. Again.

"Robert, I'm not feeling anything. I'm trying not to think about anything. I'd love to go to sleep and wake up a few weeks from now when all this has passed. I know it's not possible, but that's what I'd like."

He turned to face Robert, and then opened the door.

"I think you're right. I need to go talk to someone."

And with those words he was out the door, shutting it behind him as he left.

3

Saturday 10 pm

The chapel was empty as John suspected. He stood at the entrance, holding the door open while he made sure he wanted to go in. John knew that if he sat down on one of the pews he was going to have a conversation he might come to regret. Or worse, one that would not give him the answers he felt he needed to make sense of his life. He thought, In for a penny, in for a pound. He then closed the door behind him and sat down in the back pew.

It was not lost on him that everything had started in another hospital chapel. It was less than two weeks ago when he had prayed for Jerry to be healed and left with an assurance that God heard his prayer. He did not know then exactly how God was going to work everything out, but he trusted it would all be for the best. Sitting in the dim light of another hospital chapel he felt abandoned, seeking for answers that he wasn't sure he would find.

John knew he wasn't the first person to not understand what was happening in his life. The Psalms were filled with different writers asking God the same basic question, what's going on here? The circumstances differed from Psalm to Psalm, but the cry was basically the same, I don't understand. Many times the answer was found in the Psalm, but sometimes a Psalm was just a record of one man's cry to God for help. In those Psalms, though there was no relief found, the writer knew that hope was out there, and eventually he would find it.

Knowing all of that brought John no comfort. Everything he knew about God, that he was good, that he loved people, that his thoughts are higher than the thoughts of men, that he causes good to come from evil and suffering, none of those truths were able to answer the question that had now fully taken over his thinking. Why heal Jerry if you were just going to let him die a few days later? What's the point of a miracle if you take it away before it can bring about any good?

John usually prayed like everyone else he knew. He would bow his head and silently express his thoughts and requests to God, and then end by saying "Amen" out loud. But he was in a place he had never been before. He just looked toward the front of the chapel and started talking quietly.

"I want you to know that I'm not going to stop believing. I couldn't even if I wanted to, which I don't think I want to do. I'm not mad at you because I know it wouldn't do me any good. I've known other people who got mad at you, but I guess that's not me. I wanted to get all of that out of the way. I'm probably going to say some things that will seem pretty strong, but I guess you're big enough to take it. I know you're not going to get mad at me for what I say, so I'm just going to get it all out.

"I was so thankful when Jerry was healed. I think you know that I've been looking for a long time for you to do something big, and maybe that was wrong. I don't know why I was looking; at least I don't think I do. I didn't understand everything that happened after he was healed, but that was okay. I didn't like all of the confusion and mess that came with it; but I was willing to clean it up because I knew there was going to be good coming out of everything."

John stopped and gathered his thoughts. He had more to say but was wary of saying out loud what he was thinking. If he prayed like this in front of his board they would probably ask him to resign. Though God already knew what he was thinking and feeling, he understood that in some way he needed to hear what he was telling God. He continued,

"I don't understand why they had to die. You have to help me here. Why would you go to the trouble of healing someone and then letting them die a week later? What does that accomplish? I know he wasn't going to live forever, but a week? And Robin? She was so faithful; she hung in there through all of this. If you hadn't healed Jerry, wouldn't she still be alive? How does this help people to believe in you? How is this going to help my church? I don't want to be selfish, but what am I going to tell people? What am I going to tell Jerry's parents? Sorry your son died in an auto accident after he was miraculously healed? What do I tell the girls? That mom and dad are in heaven? I know Robin is, but Jerry? Was I wrong to pray for Jerry to be healed? Is any of this on me?"

It had been a long day. John was not only on the edge of emotional exhaustion, but he was physically spent as well. He had never had a week like this before in his life, with so many different currents pulling him in so many different directions. Now he felt he was being dragged out to sea in a riptide and fighting to stay close to shore. That fight was expressing itself in the words he was saying to God, words that he could not have imagined saying just hours before. One of those currents that left its mark on John was Mr. Banks. The thought of Mr. Banks walking around alive while Jerry and Robin were in the hospital morgue was running through his mind.

"If somebody had to die, why not Mr. Banks? No one likes him. He's wrecked the lives of his family and doesn't care about anybody but himself."

John realized he had gone too far, and knew that he was probably too tired to continue.

"Sorry. I didn't mean that. But I think you get the point. I didn't think that I would ever have a breaking point, but it's out there, and it's close. If I can't figure this out I don't know how I'm going to be good for anyone or anything. Just one more thing. Please don't answer any of my prayers for a while. Not that I will be offering many."

He didn't feel better, but he was too tired to care. He took out his phone and set the alarm for 4 am. Jerry's parents would arrive around 5 so he would at least get a few hours' sleep. The pew was cushioned, but it didn't matter. John fell asleep almost the moment he closed his eyes.

It was sunny and warm in the green meadow. There were clouds overhead that occasionally hid the sun when they wandered by. Sharon was sitting under an oak tree where there was a large blanket. The food was spread out and despite it sitting on four plates, there were no ants to bother them. John was standing about 50 yards from the tree holding a Frisbee, waiting for her to turn and look at him so he could toss it. The other girl was sitting with Sharon, talking quietly and occasionally laughing. John could not recall being so content, and then with a flick of his wrist tossed the Frisbee. It flew about 6 feet off the ground and arched slowly toward the girl. It was a good throw and as she reached out to grab it he woke up with a start. The alarm on his phone was going off, and for a moment he could not remember where he was.

He sat up in the pew, looked around and slowly his memory returned. John had slept soundly for five hours and awoke to the same reality he left when he fell asleep. He needed coffee and a chance to think about what he was going to say to Jerry's parents when they arrived. John got up from the pew, stretched for a moment to help him wake up, and then walked out the door of the chapel headed for the hospital cafeteria. It dawned on him when he stepped into the elevator that he left his phone in the chapel, sitting on the pew. He walked quickly back and found it lying there, and then headed back to the elevator and the cafeteria. There was one other thing that John forgot in the chapel. He had no memory of his dream, though it would break into his consciousness the next week, with surprising results.

4

Sunday 5 am

He was sitting in the cafeteria finishing his second cup of coffee and thinking about his night in the chapel. There was no way he could take back the words he had spoken, not that he wanted to. What was the point in believing in God if you couldn't be honest with him? Though he felt he was generally honest with God when he prayed, he had never prayed like that because he had never been in a situation like that before.

There had been other crises in his life, but he never dreaded the future as he did now. He had no answers for the questions he was going to be asked by Jerry's parents, by his church, by his board and especially the girls.

John knew he could always say that he didn't understand why these things happen but in the end God knew, and that was enough. It also had the benefit of being the truth. But that answer was dwarfed by the seeming incongruity of everything that had happened. At least it was in his mind. He knew intellectually that God was bigger than his lack of understanding. At the moment it wasn't providing him any comfort.

He was startled when his phone rang and almost spilled his coffee. It was Jerry's parents. John took a deep breath to calm himself, and then he answered. He listened for a moment, and then got up to meet them in the Emergency Room lobby.

They were sitting in the lobby looking lost and tired. They had driven most of the night from San Francisco and did not rise when John joined them. He sat down across from them and asked if they had talked to anyone yet. Jerry's father said that they were waiting for John to arrive to help them.

"Okay, let me find someone who can help us."

It did not take long for John to return with a nurse who took the three of them to the hospital morgue. The nurse explained that the funeral home would come later that morning and take the bodies back to their facility to prepare them for transport to San Francisco. She gave the parents a moment to prepare, and then opened the metal door and pulled the tray out that held Jerry's body. She pulled back the sheet so they could see his face and waited for a moment as they looked at the dead body of their only son. John wasn't surprised when there was no visible reaction. They had just driven all night and had several hours to get used to the idea that their son was gone. He was surprised, however, when they told the nurse it wasn't necessary to show them Robin's body. After the nurse returned Jerry's body to the stainless steel cooler, Jerry's dad said,

"You must have some forms we need to sign."

"We do. If you want to wait in the lobby I'll have someone come out and help you."

That's it, thought John. He followed them out to the lobby and waited until they all sat down to ask them when they might want to see their grandchildren. They looked at each other, and then the grandmother said,

"We weren't very close to our grandchildren. We've only seen them three or four times. Don't you think it's kind of late to begin a relationship with them?"

John could not believe where the conversation was headed and said to her,

"I know you guys are tired and still coming to grips with what's happened, but you're the only family these girls have. You're telling me that you don't want to see them?"

Robin's parents were both dead and though she had a younger sister, John had no idea where she lived and knew that Robin had not had any contact with her for years. His head was beginning to spin as he fought to keep his emotions under control. Jerry's father joined the conversation and said to John,

"We have discussed this at length, so we're not coming to grips with anything. Jerry had cancer and we had weeks to prepare for his death. When the cancer went into remission, we were glad for him, but always figured that it was going to come back."

"It didn't go into remission", John said. "He was healed. Brain tumors don't go into remission. I saw the x-ray and talked to the doctor. It wasn't going to come back."

Jerry's dad wasn't angry or upset. Instead, he was completely calm and spoke with an air of condescension that John found distasteful.

"Let me tell you something. We weren't happy when Jerry married her. We are not religious people and neither was Jerry. If he wanted to marry someone who felt the need to go to church, that was his choice. But it made things awkward, as you can understand."

He paused for a moment, and then continued.

"And you can't believe that your God healed Jerry. If you believe that then your God is a monster, isn't he? He would heal someone just to have them die a week later? You don't want to believe in a God like that, do you?"

John had lots of experience talking with those who did not believe in God. Most people he talked with focused on the suffering and evil that existed in the world and the fact that God allowed it to continue. If God was good, all powerful and compassionate, why didn't he intervene and do something about it? There were answers to these types of objections, though he had never argued anyone into the kingdom. What do you do with the question Jerry's father had thrown at him? John decided not to do anything with it, and asked him what was going to happen to the girls.

"We were hoping you could help us with that."

"Help how?"

"We thought they might be able to stay with you until we can get them into the system."

"Into what system?"

It turned out that Jerry's mother had worked in social services most of her career and thought the girls should first be placed in foster care, and then put up for adoption. She was confident they would be adopted together into a family, solving that problem. When she actually used the word "problem" to describe the plight of the girls, John wanted to scream. He remembered the words he had spoken just hours before when he told God he could see a breaking point out there. He was close, but just managed to hold it together.

"They can stay with us as long as necessary. You don't need to rush them into anything. It will probably take some time to look at the will and figure out what to do about their estate. Please don't worry about the girls. We'll take care of them as long as needed."

The nurse returned, telling them that the funeral home was there to pick up the bodies. Jerry's father went with the nurse to sign the forms necessary to release them. John took the opportunity to again say how sorry he was about everything. He told her there would probably be a memorial service at the church next weekend, and he hoped they might be able to attend.

"I don't think so, but thank you for asking. We'll just have to get on with our lives, I suppose."

John thought about how uncomplicated life would be if you just believed in the here and now. You lived, and then you died. It went against everything he believed and knew to be true, but sitting across from Jerry's mother, who seemed to be weathering the death of her son in a detached, clinical manner, he was almost envious. He couldn't see how hard it was for her to keep the tears from flowing. How much she regretted letting her husband keep her from her only son because he married a Christian. Also from her grandchildren, whom she would never get to know, and whom she was willing to send to live with someone unknown to her and them. That part would turn out to be untrue, but she couldn't know that then.

5

Sunday 7 am

John left the hospital at 7 and began the long drive home. He told Jerry's parents he would call them Monday and let them know how the girls were doing. Because he didn't want to think about anything he turned on the radio and listened to the news as he drove. Despite the voice of the announcer talking about local news stories, he could not keep his mind from trying to figure out how he would break the news to the girls. His concentration was broken when he heard the following words come from the radio,

"In a shocking twist of fate, a local couple died last night in a traffic accident on West Highland Boulevard. What makes this so tragic is that the husband had been discharged just a few days earlier from the hospital when his brain tumor miraculously disappeared. Some in the community claimed he was healed of his tumor. Regardless, this tragedy is sure to rock the community and especially the church the couple attended."

So it was out there, he thought. He hadn't had the time to think about the news media getting involved. It was a story they might not be able to resist. It was a shocking twist of fate, no doubt about that. How John might be dragged again into the spotlight he could not envision, unless some reporter wanted to get his reaction and fish for a good quote or sound bite.

Whether or not the tragedy would rock his church he had no idea. He knew people would have questions, just as he did, and he would have to address those questions eventually. That would come later. There was so much that was going to happen in the next few days it was making his head spin. Some was due to lack of sleep. Most of his disoriented feeling, however, was coming from the avalanche of thoughts and emotions he was struggling with. When he was less than ten miles from home he forced himself to concentrate on how he would break the news to the girls. John had never done anything like this before, though he had been involved in many deaths, subsequent funerals, and memorial services. Telling someone their relative was dead, especially children, would be much different than trying to comfort them after the fact. He finally came to the conclusion there was no easy way to do it, and resigned himself to just telling them and dealing with the aftermath.

The girls were still asleep when he walked through his front door. Sharon was in the kitchen preparing breakfast. He sat down at the table and accepted a cup of coffee from her. She sat down across from him and said,

"I kept them up late so they would sleep in. They didn't seem to mind when I told them they were going to spend the night. How did it go at the hospital?"

"It's not something I want to do again. I've seen plenty of corpses, but nothing like that. They were just lying there. I just identified the bodies and walked out."

"What were you supposed to do?"

"I don't think it's what I was supposed to do, it just caught me off guard that I didn't feel anything. I still don't."

"What about the parents? Did you get a chance to talk to them?"

"If you can call it that. It turns out they don't want to see the girls. They are going to take the bodies back to San Francisco and that's the last we'll see of them. They're not what you would call real sociable."

"What do you mean they don't want to see the girls? They are their grandchildren. They have to see them."

"You would think. They may be back when the will is probated, but they asked if we could take care of them until they can make arrangements to put them into foster care. I told them we would watch them as long as necessary."

John left out the comments made by Jerry's dad concerning Robin and their rejection of her based on her Christian faith. He also did not mention the remark about how John could believe in a God who would heal someone and then let them die a week later. He continued,

"I can get help from the church to watch the girls. I know it's a lot to spring on you, but I thought it would be best if the girls stayed with us."

"That's not a problem. I can take some vacation until we get this sorted out."

There was silence as both of them thought about how events were going to unfold. Uppermost in John's mind was still the girls and how much longer they were going to sleep. He had to tell them soon after they were up because it would prove impossible to shield them from what was going to happen. The phone calls, the people coming to visit and who knew what else. John also thought about the church service that was going to begin soon. He knew that the news of a member dying suddenly, especially when they were so young, would be the talk of the church for weeks. Some would want to help, some would want more information and those who knew Robin well would have to find ways to grieve. At that moment John knew he was not up to the task of leading the church through any of that.

Sharon's thoughts were heading in another direction entirely. She too was thinking about the girls, but not about when they were going to wake up. She wasn't even thinking about how they were going to tell them their parents were dead. The thought of putting them into foster care had sparked a thought that would have been completely foreign to her just a week or so earlier. She knew it wasn't the right time to share it with John, so she kept it to herself. John took a sip of his coffee, looked down at the table, and said in a low voice,

"I need to tell you that I'm close to the edge right now. I've never felt like this before, and at the moment I don't see how I'm going to be able to function. I can't get my mind to slow down and, uh, I can't feel anything. It's like everything is behind a dam and slowly building, giving me all this pressure. I keep waiting for it to break, but it just keeps building. I don't know what to do."

Sharon wanted to tell him what he already knew, that somehow God would help him through this time of difficulty. That God could bring good out of this tragedy and though answers at the moment seemed out of reach, they would come with time. It was not lost on her how quickly the tables had turned in their relationship. Just last week it was John trying to help her deal with issues that haunted her for years. Her eyes had been opened to see things that were hidden from her most of her life, especially in regards to her father. Now she was the one who was in the position of trying to help her spouse find a way out of a really dark place. She didn't want to offer advice, but she thought of one thing that might be appropriate.

"Maybe we should pray about all this. I think that would help both of us."

Before John could answer they heard noises coming from down the hallway. They both knew that the girls were up and that the time had come to bring them the news about their parents. John turned to Sharon and said,

"Let's give them breakfast first."

It was Sharon who told them about their parents. After breakfast they took the girls to the living room and Sharon took her time breaking the news to them. It took Kendra, the six year old, a few minutes to realize she wasn't going to see her mommy and daddy again. Allison, the eight year old, understood almost immediately and began to softly cry. When Kendra finally understood what had happened, she too began to cry. Sharon sat on the couch between them and put her arms around their shoulders. John was across from them in a chair. As he watched and listened he could not help but feel detached from it all. He felt for the girls, but he knew what he was feeling wasn't the sorrow he would normally experience in that type of situation. When Sharon told the girls that she and John would take care of them and help them, he did not notice the feeling and compassion in her voice.

When the girls were finally cried out, Sharon suggested that they lie on the couch and watch a movie together. It served as a temporary distraction, and there would be more crying off and on during the day. John would go over to their house to get the girls some clothes and toys. He was given Jerry's keys at the hospital and left soon after the movie started. As he drove there was one thought that came to him from the conversation he had with Jerry's mother. She said they really didn't have a relationship with their grandchildren. So far the children had not mentioned the grandparents at all. They were certainly out of the picture, leaving John and Sharon to deal with two young kids whose parents had just been taken from them. Fortunately for them, they would prove equal to the task. It would take John time to get there, but he would, after a short but painful journey.

He would find the time later in the day to take a short but much needed nap. Around 3 Sharon took the girls out to play and then for some ice cream. They needed a diversion, something to get their minds off the calamity that had befallen them. They would spend the next week with Sharon, who took them out of school. Though there would continue to be times of grief and sadness for months to come, they would slowly find a new normal that would bring some stability back into their lives.

John fell asleep soon after they left. For the second time that weekend he had a vivid dream. He was again standing in the green meadow with the sun shining overhead and a warm breeze moving the leaves of the big oak tree. This time he was alone though he did not feel the aloneness. He looked around at the beauty of his surroundings and was content just to stand there and take it all in.

After an indeterminate amount of time he began to walk toward the only distinguishing feature in the meadow, the oak tree. When he was about twenty feet away he noticed a large book lying against the trunk. He looked around to see if the book might belong to someone, but he was still the only person in the meadow. As he stood there the contentment that he felt was slowly being replaced by fear, a fear he knew was associated with the book. He looked around again, and satisfied he was alone, walked up to the tree and picked up the book. It was large and heavy in his hands and he knew why he was becoming afraid. If he opened the book, there would be words that would reach out and grab at his heart, and he knew that was what frightened him. He woke up when he heard Sharon pull into the driveway and like the previous night, he would have no memory of his dream. Though he had slept, he was not in any way refreshed.

6

Monday 7.30 am

He was at the office early Monday morning. He had to begin to sort out what he absolutely needed to do to keep the church functioning. There was a memorial service to plan. He had to think about the next Sunday service. He would have to talk with Jerry's parents. He had a scheduled board meeting on Thursday he would love to postpone. Both he and Sharon had turned off their phones on Sunday to give them a chance to deal with the kids. John needed a break before starting what was sure to be a stressful week. When he turned it on at the office there were only four messages, one from Edward, two from board members and the last from Jerry's parents. They had called Sunday night to let him know they had been to the house to get Jerry's and Robin's will and would have the lawyer who wrote it get back to John with any information related to the girls.

He didn't bother to listen to the other messages; he simply deleted them without any afterthought. John would talk to the board later in the week, so they could wait. Edward was another story. The first thing he did when he got up that morning was send Edward a text telling him he would be at his office until noon and to come by sometime before then. He wanted to know about the service; what happened, what was the reaction of the church, how many visitors were there and what if anything Edward did with them.

John had not looked at any emails in two days and thought he better take a glance at what had accumulated. As he looked down his inbox he saw that most of them were pretty standard, there didn't seem to be any out of the ordinary. Until he came to the most recent, which had just been sent that morning. It was from an address he did not recognize with a subject line that read, Don't pray for me. He opened the email and read the following short sentence, Please don't pray for me, I don't want to die. It was not signed and the email address was not in the form of a name, so he had no way of knowing who sent it. He knew that his email address was on the church website, so the message could have come from anyone who knew that Jerry and Robin had died.

There was no point in responding, someone was just trying to provoke him. John also knew if there was one person thinking that way there were sure to be others. He suspected the email was from someone outside the church, but he had no way of knowing for sure. His hand was moving the cursor toward the delete button when he decided instead to print the email. If he deleted the message it would be gone. If he printed it he would have a permanent record to remind him of what others thought of Jerry's and Robin's death. Without hesitating he hit "print" and waited for his printer to come to life and give him the anonymous email. After it printed he sat it on his desk and then instead of deleting the message, forwarded it to his board. He didn't know why he sent it to them; it just felt like the right thing to do. It wasn't, but he wouldn't find that out until he met with the board on Thursday.

Just then Edward walked into the outer office. John saw him through the glass in his door and motioned for him to enter his office. Edward sat down across from John and waited for him to say something. Edward didn't know how to begin a conversation where so much had happened in less than forty-eight hours. So they both waited, which did not bother John in the least, but was making Edward slightly uncomfortable. The spell that was developing was broken when the church phone suddenly sprang to life. Edward jumped in response while John merely turned his head to look at the caller ID on the phone's display screen. When he saw it was the television station that interviewed him just over a week ago, he took the receiver off the hook and then gently sat it down, ending the call. He then pulled the telephone line out of the phone, ensuring that anyone who called would get a busy signal. John looked at Edward and said,

"The blood is in the water and the sharks are hungry."

It took Edward a moment to get the meaning of John's words.

"The news media?"

"The same station that I talked with after Jerry was healed. Probably thinking this would make a great story on the news tonight. Let's ask the pastor why the man he healed died a week later. With his wife. Leaving two orphans. What do you have to say about that pastor?"

There was more than a touch of sarcasm in John's voice and Edward also noticed he looked terrible. He guessed that John hadn't slept much and was carrying a burden that had aged him since Edward had last seen him.

"I don't think that most people are thinking that. It's a tragedy that no one could have foreseen."

"Oh, I think there's one person who could have foreseen it."

Edward understood what John was saying and had no idea how to respond. While he was thinking John took a piece of paper on his desk and handed it to Edward. Edward read the one line and then set in back on the desk.

"This isn't your fault."

"Let's say that's true. Whose fault do you think it is?"

"Maybe it's no one's fault. Maybe things just happen because the world is a fallen place that's filled with tragedies like this."

It wasn't an answer that was going to satisfy John, and Edward knew it.

"So you're saying that God could not have prevented this? That it was just something random? That it doesn't relate to anything else God might have done?"

It was scary to watch John pose these questions without any visible emotion. He had obviously been thinking about nothing else since Saturday night and was giving Edward a look into his mind, but not his heart.

"John, if God prevented every tragedy or suffering, we would never experience his comfort or find the good that can come out of tragedy. I know you understand this, and have probably said it others when they're suffering."

"I'm not asking God to change the way he works. I just think he could have prevented this from happening. Kind of makes him look like a monster, doesn't it. Takes away cancer, something really good, and then takes away the life of the person he just healed. And his wife."

Edward was about to respond when John said,

"I get that there is suffering. I get that tragedy is all around us. I just don't get this. And I don't know that I ever will."

"You wanted God to do something big, and he did. Nothing has turned out the way you thought it would when you asked God to heal Jerry. You told me that we ought to be willing to walk toward the messes instead of walking away. This certainly qualifies as a mess. Why not trust God and walk toward the mess instead of trying to figure it out?"

Then Edward said something that took the conversation in a completely different direction, and when it was over he would be without a job.

"I know you can get past this."

He wanted to add the phrase, because God is bigger than our hurts, but John sat up in his chair and said,

"You don't know anything of the kind. You have no idea how close I am to running out of this office and never coming back."

"You could do that, but you know it wouldn't solve anything. You have people that need you and are going to look to you for leadership to get through this. I know it's going to sound trite, but we have to trust God in times like this. He's all that we have."

There was no way their time together was going to end well. It would have been better if Edward had just let John talk and not try to answer his questions or deal with his pain. Edward was young and had not yet learned that sometimes people just need to say what they are thinking or feeling and leave it at that. John leaned forward from his chair and put his hands on his desk, and then said to Edward,

"So you trust that God can take care of us in any situation. No matter what happens?"

"Yeah, I believe that."

John nodded his head, and then said something that he would immediately regret, but not retract.

"Good. Then you believe that God will take care of you when I fire you right now. Correct?"

John wasn't kidding, and Edward knew it. He also knew he had pushed John too far and just needed to leave. He didn't care whether he was fired or not, he just hoped John would eventually find his way back to some sort of spiritual sanity. He stood up to leave and said in parting,

"I'm sorry. If you change your mind, call me."

Then he was out of the office, closing the door softly behind him.

John immediately knew he had acted rashly. One part of him cared, another part felt the thrill of doing something that was completely spontaneous and out of character for him. That thrill slowly dissipated as he sat in his chair and watched Edward walk across the parking lot to his car. He had never done anything like that before in his life, and at that moment he didn't even know who he was or what he might become.

Despite what Edward said to him, John didn't see any way he was going to get out of the spiral he was in. For ten years as a pastor he had been there for others. He helped people through their difficulties, temptations, broken relationships, sins and addictions. He knew if the roles were reversed, he would have told Edward exactly what Edward had told him. John also knew that Edward was probably right when he said he would be able to get past this. He also knew that he was so far away from having the strength to face even his next responsibility that he felt nothing but confusion and defeat. He could talk to Robert, but he knew Robert was going to need time to recover from his surgery. Sharon had just been given the responsibility to care for the two girls and was still coming to grips with some of her past. His board would be sympathetic but he doubted that he could speak candidly to them about what he was going through. He took out his phone, brought up his contacts and pressed the first name on the list. He waited until he heard a voice on the other end, and then said,

"I really need to see you today."

7

Monday 10 am

Amy was free that morning so John left his office and was sitting across from her in less than an hour after talking with Edward. She heard about the accident Sunday morning and was thinking how it was going to affect John. When he called that morning she was glad she could immediately see him. He did not look good, and sat down without any greeting or small talk. They sat in silence until John said,

"Jerry and I were supposed to meet this week to talk about his relationship with God."

John was looking out her office window and seemed to be talking to himself. Amy thought about how to begin a dialogue with him, and responded by saying,

"How are the girls doing?"

"Let's see. Their mom and dad are dead. Their grandparents don't want to have anything to do with them. Their only other relative could be anywhere on the planet. I guess it could be worse."

"How could it be worse?"

"They haven't asked me yet why God would heal their daddy and then have him die a week later."

So it was out on the table. Amy knew she would have to be careful what she said in the next few minutes. She guessed that John had thought about little else since the accident. She could tell he was close to the edge emotionally.

"What would you tell them if they did ask?"

"I have no idea Amy. What would you tell them?"

For the first time since he sat down he turned and looked her in the face. Though he asked her about the girls, she knew that he was the one looking for an answer. She could give him an answer, but it would be one he was familiar with. He certainly had used it in his own counseling with those who were going through difficult circumstances. Before she had a chance to reply, John said,

"What do I tell them if they ask if their daddy is in heaven? I never even got the chance to talk with Jerry about his relationship with God."

"Are you looking for someone to blame? That would be natural because it would give you someone to be angry with. Right now you're drowning because your emotions have nowhere to go."

He knew she was right; he was looking for someone to blame. There were really only two candidates, and the consequences of blaming one or the other would leave him completely devastated. She interrupted his train of thought when she asked him,

"What if there's no one to blame? I know it helps to have someone to blame when things go wrong. Then we know who to be angry with. Then we have someone to point to and say, "You're a bad person, you did this". But I'm not sure that we can do that every time there are tragedies in life."

She was going to say something John had heard before. He rejected it then because of who said it. This time he would listen and would react in a completely different manner. Amy said,

"This isn't your fault.

She paused for a moment, and then added,

"It's not his fault either."

He knew it wasn't his fault, but that left John with only one alternative. One that he could not admit to himself.

"Let's pretend for a moment what you say is true. What's the point of healing Jerry and then letting him die? You and I both know that he could have prevented this even if he didn't cause it."

John emphasized the word "letting" when he spoke, and then waited for Amy's answer. He was trying to put her in the loop that had caused him to fire Edward, the loop that kept running through his mind and was giving him no rest. The loop he could not find an answer to.

"What if I gave you an answer that was absolutely correct, one that you knew was true. One that satisfied your mind. Would you walk out of here feeling differently than when you came in?"

"Let's find out. Do you have an answer you think I'll buy? Give me your best shot."

"Okay. Here's my answer." She paused for a moment, and then said, "I don't know."

At least Edward had tried to give him an answer. That good can come out of evil. That suffering helps us know God better.

"Even if it's true, I can't tell people that there isn't an answer. It would make me look like an idiot. I can't do it. I can't."

Amy had known John long enough to know he wasn't a vain person. He had dealt with a lot in his life, but nothing like this. He was the leader of a growing church; he had helped many people deal with their own problems and suffering. He stood in front of people telling them what God thought, what the Bible said, and how to live and make sense of life. John just didn't have it in him to say to others, in the wake of the biggest tragedy he would likely ever know, I don't have a clue. Amy took a chance and went straight to what he had just said.

"You're worrying about yourself here, John. You're thinking about how you're going to come across if you tell people you don't understand why this happened. This isn't about you."

"You're wrong, Amy. This is all about me. It's my responsibility to try and explain what God is like, how much he loves people, how to know him. If I stand up and tell people I have no clue why Jerry and Robin are dead, what are they going to think about God?"

John spoke with some heat, so Amy lowered her voice and slowly said,

"John, God doesn't need you to defend him. He can take care of his own reputation. You shouldn't worry so much about yours."

He looked at her for a moment and wanted to respond, "How can you understand what I worry about?" Amy's husband had been a pastor, so she knew all too well what it was like to be the leader of a church where people expected you to have the answer to any question they might have.

"There is another part of the answer I gave you. It's really not complete without putting the two parts together. I think it's okay to say we don't understand as long as we also say we trust God, who does understand. I know you may not be there yet, but I know that you will be, even if it takes some time."

He had fired Edward when he spoke the same words to him. That he could get past this. When he thought of what he had done, that he had rejected from Edward what he was now willing to accept from Amy, and acted rashly by firing him, he started to weep. Since Saturday night he was racing toward this, a time when he needed to give up trying to think his way out of a tragedy that had no straightforward, rational explanation.

It was not unusual for people to cry in Amy's office. They came to her to talk about the difficulties they were having in life, and many times as Amy tried to help them, tears would flow. She couldn't remember, though, seeing anyone as broken as John, who sat with his head in his hands for several minutes sobbing uncontrollably. She reached for a box of tissue she kept on her desk and sat it in front of him. He finally straightened up, took a few tissues, wiped his eyes, and said,

"You're not going to bill me for this, are you?"

She laughed and knew that John had most likely turned a corner, though it would take time to get through the grief and heartache of Jerry and Robin's death.

"I want to tell you something else."

"What's that?"

"Something good is going to come out of this. I don't know what, but God will bring something good from this."

8

Monday 11 am

As he drove back to his office, John knew there were still questions that would haunt him for perhaps the rest of his life. He needed to get the questions that were running through his mind out in the open so he could deal with the emotions that were just below the surface. Amy told him things he already knew but did not have the ability to admit. The bottom line was that John was not going to stop believing because of a tragedy he could not explain. He never thought he would be in a place where he would be at a loss to understand what was happening to him. He certainly never thought he would fall apart as he did in Amy's office.

As a pastor, it had taken him time to learn he could not fix people. They came to him with their difficulties, brokenness and sins, and as he listened he tried to guide them to solutions they could find for themselves. He might tell them what he would do in their circumstance, but he found that if he told people what to do they would invariably stop coming to see him. Amy was wise enough to let him talk about what was eating him up and then offer a few thoughts for him to think through. Mainly, he just needed to let someone hear what he was going through and give him a safe place to release the grief and anger he had been holding inside.

John ran his cell phone through his car's Bluetooth so he could talk hands free while he drove. He was getting close to church when his phone rang. It was the church office, and John hesitated for a moment before answering. He pressed a button on his steering wheel to answer, and then said,

"Hi Susan. What can I do for you??"

"I have a reporter from the newspaper here who would like to speak with you. Will you be in soon?"

He had no desire to talk with any reporter. He had the thought, however, that the questions a reporter would ask would be the same as what others were going to bring to him.

"I'll be there in about ten minutes if she wants to wait."

His phone rang again and he saw that it was Mr. Banks. He told Susan he had another call and let her go, then connected to Mr. Banks.

"Good morning Mr. Banks."

"I wonder how you're doing today."

"Why would you care about how I'm doing?"

"I talked to Sharon this morning. She called to see how her mother is feeling."

"Why would you talk to Sharon? Has something happened to her mother?"

"Yes."

Mr. Banks paused for a moment so John might think the worst. Then he said,

"She is much better. The doctor left this morning saying he has never seen anyone get better so fast with this type of condition."

He spoke with an assurance that John found distasteful. He was glad and surprised that Mrs. Banks was doing better, but knew exactly why Mr. Banks had called.

"I'm happy she's feeling better."

Before he could continue, Mr. Banks interrupted him and said,

"No thanks to you, of course. You wouldn't bother to pray for her, even when you knew she was dying. But God heard my prayer after all."

Then he paused for a moment, and said,

"I guess you won't be praying for any more people to be healed, will you?"

So Mr. Banks had heard about the accident. John could imagine the smile on Mr. Banks face and hear the gloating in his voice. Mr. Banks called John with the intention of causing him pain and doubt, but he had already been there and was now very slowly coming back.

"Mr. Banks, is there something I can do for you? If not, I'm almost back at my office and need to get back to work."

He pulled into the church parking lot and guided his car into a space close to the front door. John let the engine idle as he waited for Mr. Banks to respond.

"I wonder why you would be going to your office. I would think you would be writing your resignation."

He would later regret continuing the conversation, but couldn't help himself at the moment. The thought of resigning had never occurred to him, though he could understand why Mr. Banks would bring the subject up.

"Mr. Banks, I haven't done anything wrong. Why would I resign?"

"Your pride has caused the death of two people in your church. Pride is the worst sin a preacher can have. You should repent of your sin and resign."

He felt he was being dragged into a conversation he wanted no part of but was unable to resist.

"What pride?"

"The idea that you knew who God wanted to heal. The pride that you could think he would listen to you because you're better than everyone else. The pride you showed when you were on the television and in the newspaper. I guess you don't feel so proud now."

"You're right about one thing. I don't feel so proud right now, but not in the way you might think. I thought I understood some things about God, but I find I still have plenty to learn. I thought I understood why God healed Jerry, but now I don't know. I thought I was stronger than I turned out to be, but I found out I was wrong about that, too. You're right, pride is a terrible thing."

Mr. Banks was goading John, hoping to get him to lash out in anger or at least lose his composure. When John was finished speaking, Mr. Banks had nothing left to say, and ended the conversation.

The one thing John took away from the conversation was that Mrs. Banks was feeling better. He didn't care why she was better or whose prayer was responsible. He was just happy that Sharon was being spared a burden she wouldn't have to carry.

He took a few deep breaths to collect himself, and then walked into the outer office. Susan and a woman sitting on the couch stood up as he entered.

"Good morning pastor. This is Sheila Morris. She's from the newspaper."

John extended his hand in greeting and said,

"Why don't you come into my office?"

She followed him and sat down across from the desk. She reached into her purse and took out a notebook that she casually opened. She began innocently enough.

"I'm sorry about the accident. How are the two little girls doing?"

"As you might guess, they are missing their mom and dad. We're keeping them out of school this week and trying to keep them busy. There's no doubt they are going through a lot of grief and pain."

"You said "we're". Where are they living right now?"

"They're staying with my wife and I until we get some things figured out."

"They don't have any family?"

"Their only relatives live up north and they decided for the time being it would be easier if the girls stayed with us. We've known them most of their lives."

The reporter was writing in her notebook and then asked, without looking up,

"What does your church think about what's happened? Have any of them lost faith?"

"Why would anyone here lose faith? This isn't the first tragedy we've faced together as a church."

"But don't you think this is different?"

John knew where she wanted to go, but was not going to help her get there. He wanted her to ask him directly, and he said so.

"Why don't you ask me the questions you really want to ask?"

"I'm sorry?"

"You want to ask me why would God heal somebody then let them die. Something like that."

"Yes. Something like that."

"I don't know."

"What don't you know?"

"That's my answer. I don't know."

"It's not much of an answer. Is that what you're going to tell your church?"

"As a matter of fact, it is."

"You don't think that might cause people to question their belief in God? That he could allow something like this to happen to someone you claimed he had just healed?"

"Ma'am, there's no doubt God healed Jerry. You can ask his doctor."

"I think you're missing the point. What's the use of healing someone if they're just going to die a week later?"

"Like I said, I don't know the answer to that specific question."

He reached into his briefcase and took out his Bible. He sat it on the desk and the pushed it toward the reporter.

"It says in this book that God is good. That God loves people. That good can come out of suffering and tragedy. I believe that, though to some it may seem silly to do so."

She had enough for her story and thanked him for his time. He stood and watched her leave and then sat back down in his chair.

Susan came in through the open door and asked him how he was doing.

"Better than I was this morning. Could you get Edward on the phone for me?"

9

Wednesday 5 pm

Sharon called him at the church office and said they needed to go see her mother that evening. She had arranged for a lady at the church to come and watch the girls. Sharon did not give John a reason though he thought it must have something to do with the change in her mother's health. He did not feel comfortable using the word "healed" until he saw her. He knew from the last time he was with her there was no way she was going to get better with anything short of a miracle.

He picked Sharon up at home and went inside to see the girls. They were having some difficulty sleeping through the night, but were slowly finding a way to manage their grief. Sharon told them she would be back later with a surprise and gave them each a hug before John walked with her to the car.

"This will be the fourth time in two weeks that I've talked with your dad. Must be some kind of record."

"I want you to stay in the car. I need to speak to him alone."

"Okay. But why am I going if I'm staying in the car? You think you might need back up?"

"Maybe. I might need help when I bring my mother out to the car."

"Bring your mother out to the car? Why would you bring her out to the car?"

Sharon was silent as John pulled onto the freeway. He thought for a moment and then said,

"Don't you think you should have asked me? It's not a decision I would have made without asking you."

"I know how you feel about my father and how trapped my mother has been all of her life. I didn't think you would have any objection. You don't, do you?"

"No, as a matter of fact, I don't. But you know your dad is going to go ballistic. He's under the impression he healed your mother. The last thing he expects is that she's going to leave him. How did all this come about anyway?"

"I called her today to see how she was doing. When she said she was off the oxygen and feeling fine, I knew that God was giving her a chance to have some happiness and peace in her life. I told her she needed to come and stay with us for a while, and she agreed."

"A while?"

"Well, maybe longer than a while. I'm going to need her help with the kids when I go back to work. I think she would be a great grandmother, don't you?"

"What do you mean, "Grandmother"?

Sharon turned to him as he drove and smiled. He glanced over and saw that she had an impish grin on her face, one that he had never seen before.

"It turns out that Jerry's will was drawn up by one of the lawyers in my firm. He was looking it over today after he was contacted by Jerry's parents and called me into his office. It seems that Jerry and Robin changed their will three months ago and made us guardians of their children. They hadn't got around to telling us, though that won't matter to the court."

It was taking a moment for everything to become clear to John. His first thought went back to the dream where he was standing in the meadow throwing the Frisbee to a little girl. Sharon sitting under a tree with another little girl having lunch without a care in the world. Then he thought of Amy's last words to him. That something good was going to come out of this. Finally, he knew God had been listening to his prayer for a child and had been waiting for the right time to answer. There was much he still did not understand, and would perhaps never understand, but that was okay. He was going to be a father.

"John? What are you thinking?"

He kept his eyes on the road, blinking several times to keep the tears from blurring his vision. He shook his head slowly to indicate that he didn't know what to say, and then shrugged his shoulders.

"It took me most of the afternoon to come to grips with all this. That's when I knew I had to get my mother out of there. It all made sense to me, all at once. I'm not looking forward to talking to my father, but it's something I have to do."

They drove the rest of the way in silence, and when they arrived at her parent's home Sharon hesitated for a moment, and then got out of the car. She said,

"Don't worry. I'll be alright. I shouldn't be too long."

He watched her walk up to the house and knock lightly on the door. It was still light and John could see Mr. Banks walk past the living room window to open the door. When the door opened he could see the two of them talking, and then Mr. Banks moved aside so Sharon could enter. Before he closed the door behind her he took a long look at John, who smiled and waved at him and said to himself,

"Boy is your world about to change."

Sharon waited until her father closed the door, and then asked him to sit down in the living room. He sat down in a chair and she sat across from him on the couch, and said,

"Now that mother is feeling better, I think it would be a good idea if she came to visit with us for a while. I talked with her this afternoon and she agrees."

"What do you mean? We can't leave and stay with you."

So typical, she thought. He heard only what he wanted to hear. The thought that his wife would go somewhere without him was inconceivable.

"I didn't say you, I said her. I'm taking her to live with me for a while."

She had changed from "visit" to "live" on purpose so that he would understand what was happening.

"What are you talking about? She is not leaving to go live with you. Where did this come from?"

"From me, actually. I need her help now that I have two young girls to take care of."

His reaction was similar to John's; it was too much for him to take in all at once. Except in his case it was not a reaction that resulted in joy, but one that was going to leave him angry and bitter.

"What do you mean you have two girls to take care of? Are you talking about the man who died? His children?"

"Yes, the man who died. With his wife. They have made us guardians of their children."

"You can't take your mother. She needs to stay with me. I won't allow it. She's my wife. You just can't come here and take her away. It's not right."

Sharon stood up from the couch and moved toward her father. Though she recently had come to see how he had robbed her of much joy and happiness in her life, she spoke slowly, deliberately and kept her emotions in check.

"I'm going to tell you what's not right. It's not right that you have marginalized her for most of her life. It's not right that you have treated her like a servant rather than a companion. It's not right that you had expectations for your children they could never achieve. It's not right that you left us with the impression that to be happy was somehow sinful. It's not right that you let your children think that God is only happy with them when they obey and then leave them thinking they can never be obedient enough to make him happy. I can't begin to tell you all the things that aren't right with you."

No one, with the exception of John, had ever talked to him in such a manner. He had lived for so long controlling nearly everyone around him and setting the tone of every conversation that he was momentarily at a loss for words. Sharon waited a moment for him to respond, and then began to move toward the stairs. She stopped when he got up from his chair and said,

"You can't take her. The only reason she's better is that I prayed for her. If you take her away from me you're responsible for what happens to her."

"There's no risk in doing what's right. I think the best thing for my mother is to come and live with my family. You're the only one who would think that God would punish her for trying to find a measure of happiness in her life by being with family members that will love and respect her."

Sharon turned and walked up the stairs, leaving her dad fuming in the living room. There was a part of him that could not accept what was about to happen and another part that was trying to figure out how to prevent his wife from leaving. It did not take him long to realize that he was helpless to stop the chain of events that were unfolding. Moments later Sharon and Mrs. Banks came down the stairs and stepped into the living room. Sharon was carrying a suitcase while her mother, who looked years younger than the last time Sharon had seen her, held a small purse in her hand. She looked at her husband of 45 years and said,

"Please be sure to feed the cat. His food is under the sink."

With the realization that his wife was actually going to leave him hitting him full in the face, Mr. Banks said,

"What's going to happen to me?"

Sharon seldom went to the movies, didn't watch much TV and had never uttered a swear word in her life. But she had seen "Gone with the Wind", and a line from the movie ran through her head.

"Frankly, I don't give a damn."

Sharon tried not to smile, but to no avail. If she thought her father was going to make one last attempt to stop his wife from leaving, she was wrong. They walked out the front door and toward the car where John was waiting. He opened the back door for Mrs. Banks and said to her,

"Welcome to the family."

10

Thursday 7 pm

John had not seen Edward since Monday but had talked with him on the phone. Their conversation was brief and to the point. Edward willingly accepted John's apology and came back to work on Thursday. John spent Tuesday and Wednesday planning the memorial and thinking about the Sunday service. Thursday afternoon he was at the beach with Sharon and the girls before heading back to his office. They were trying to get the girls out of the house each day to keep their minds off of the grief that was always just below the surface. John made a few trips to the house to get clothes and toys, but both of them thought it was too soon to take them back to their former home.

John didn't have an agenda for the board meeting, which was unusual. He sent out an email explaining that he thought it was important they meet together to talk about the events of the past week. As he planned the memorial service and had to relive Jerry and Robin's death, he found the questions that haunted him were still lurking in his mind. He knew what he wanted to say at the service, and hoped it would convey to those who came what he was beginning to understand about God and how he works through tragedy.

He was the last one to arrive at the conference room, which was also unusual. John didn't want to have to sit through any small talk;

he wanted to get right into the meeting. They were seated around the large table talking in low tones when John came through the door.

"Sorry I'm late. As you can imagine, the last few days have been difficult and I've been sort of overwhelmed. I thought it was important we talk about what's happened and see how everyone is doing."

Randy was the first to ask John how he was coping, and if there was any way they might be able to help him.

"It's been a roller coaster for me, as I suspect it's been for some of you. It took me several days to get through everything I was feeling. I did and said some stupid things, but I think God understands all that. I will say that I still don't understand everything that's happened and I'm trying to move away from actively looking for an answer. What little faith I have tells me that God understands and for now that's enough."

There was silence in the room as the men thought about what John had said. It was broken when Michael asked,

"What are we going to tell the church? You know, about the accident? We sort of left everyone hanging last week."

"I've been thinking about that. I know we have to say something because the circumstances are so unique. I know you have probably seen the newspaper article that came out yesterday. I didn't have a neat and tidy answer for the reporter, and I don't have a neat and tidy answer for our church. I understand that saying "I don't know" to people may not be very satisfying, but right now that's where I'm at."

"After what happened last time, why would you talk to a reporter?"

"I thought about that, I really did. But I knew the questions a reporter would ask would be questions that other people would be thinking. Plus, if you say "no" to a reporter it gives them the opportunity to write whatever they want without your input."

Michael had another agenda he wanted to bring out, so he continued by saying,

"Do you think God may be trying to tell us something else here?"

John knew where Michael wanted to go, and was disappointed that he would share his own fears and assumptions in the meeting. Michael wanted to get the church back to the way it was before Jerry was healed, and saw an opening that he might exploit.

"I think there might be lots of things God might want us to learn, but my guess is that you have something specific in mind."

"Do you think it's a good idea continuing to emphasize healing in view of what has happened?"

Fear is a terrible thing, John thought. Michael was not a manipulative person, but like many Christians he was held captive by his fears. In his case, it was the fear of the unknown, of what else might happen in the church if God continued to heal people. He liked the results, but not the method. His heart could be touched by people's suffering, and he felt for their pain. His fear, however, that the church would become something alien to him caused him to question what John was willing to accept.

"You think that God might be telling us it was a mistake to pray for Jerry to be healed? Is that what you're saying?"

"Maybe not for Jerry to be healed, but to make it a part of the church. I'm not the only one who thinks this."

"So you're thinking that God healed Jerry and then allowed him to die so we wouldn't pray for anyone else to be healed? Is that what you mean?"

The way John phrased the question made it sound as ridiculous as it was. Michael stiffened in his chair and his face turned slightly red. It was Edward who jumped into the conversation to keep it from getting out of hand.

"I know that I'm new to the church but I've been through this before. I told John about something that happened to me a few years ago, something similar to this."

He took a few minutes to tell them the story of the man who was healed in Mexico and the aftermath. When he finished Randy asked,

"How does that relate to what's happened here? What do you want us to take from that?"

"I learned that God will do what he wants. Sometimes it's because we pray, sometimes not. I learned that when you ask God to do something big, like heal someone, it may not turn out the way you think. I learned that God sometimes answers by creating a bigger mess than the one I was praying for. I am learning those messes are what God uses to challenge and shape our faith. I think that in this case we need to walk toward the mess instead of trying to walk away from it."

Edward understood how his words would be taken by Michael. He was literally the new kid on the block and had no real standing among the board. They may have liked him, but it wasn't even normal that he would attend a board meeting. Let alone contradict a board member. He figured he didn't have anything to lose by sharing his thoughts. He had already been fired and rehired that week; he really didn't care what might happen to him. As soon as he was finished, Michael replied,

"Well this certainly qualifies as a mess, that's for sure."

It was too much for Wayne, who had been hit hard by Jerry and Robin's death. His kids were about the same age and his wife and Robin had been good friends.

"I don't think it's appropriate to talk about what happened as a "mess". I don't understand any of this either, but I'm not willing to say I've got a line on what God wants us to do in the church because of this. I do know that he wants us to take care of the kids and help others who may be grieving. Just don't tell me you know what God thinks about any of this. Because you don't."

The meeting could have easily got out of control at that point. John was thinking back to when he identified the bodies and the conversation with Jerry's parents. He was thinking about the questions that were still hiding in the recesses of his mind. He was reliving the conversation in the hospital chapel where he expressed his frustration to God. And he was thinking about how inadequate he felt to stand in front of others in a few days and try to give hope or encouragement.

He brought them back to the point when he said,

"Guys, I know you have lots of questions and concerns. I don't have a lot of answers. Can we agree to trust God and focus on helping those in our church to get through this difficult time?"

"I think the question is how we're going to help, not if we're going to help."

Tim had finally joined the conversation and wanted to know, just like Michael, if John was going to continue what they saw as his emphasis on healing. John knew they would not be satisfied until he answered their question.

"I'm going to continue to give people the opportunity to receive prayer after the Sunday service. I don't know that it will focus on healing, but if people show up and want us to pray for them, that's what we're going to do."

"Even after what happened to Jerry? You don't think that might be a bad idea?"

John looked around at the faces of the men in the room. He was not going to change Tim or Michael's mind, but he might be able to get them to think differently if he involved them in the process.

"Tim, I think it would be appropriate if you and the rest of the guys joined me in this. I know that you care about people. I know that you have compassion for people. I know you have followed Jesus for many years and have great faith. I believe your prayers would bless and help people no matter what their need. What do you think? Will you help me?"

What was he going to say? That he wasn't going to pray for people? That he didn't care about people in need? That he wasn't willing to let God use him? Before he could answer, Randy said,

"I'll pray with you, John. I don't have a lot of faith, but I'm willing to let God use me if he wants."

Wayne and Edward both joined Randy in affirming they would help in any way John wanted. It was a big step for both men. They were going way outside their comfort zone, but not Edward. He had been down this road before, and as he told the group, was willing to walk toward the mess instead of away from it. Michael and Tim, however, were not swayed in their opinion, though Tim had doubts.

Tim was torn as he listened to the three men talk about their willingness to follow John. He knew there was truth in what John was saying, and part of him longed to see God use him in the way John was describing. But he was afraid, and he knew it. When he finally answered John's question, he was surprised at his own honesty. He spoke slowly and would not make eye contact with John.

"If that's the direction you want to take the church, I'm probably not going to stay on the board. I understand what you're saying; it's just not in me to change in the way you want. I'm sorry."

John could feel the conflict in Tim. He said to him,

"I get that it's hard to change. I get that, I really do. I don't think you need to leave the board just because you have a difference of opinion, but that's your choice. But I would like you to wait a month before you do anything. Maybe you'll have a change of heart. You never know."

The meeting ended on that note. John would meet with Tim several times in the next few weeks and not only convince him to stay on the board, but help him deal with some of the issues in his life that contributed to his fear. He would not be as successful with Michael. Michael and Susan would leave the church in the coming months, and John would again have to look for another staff member. The search didn't take long because he brought in Sharon's mother, who knew how churches worked from being a pastor's wife for so many years. She would drop the girls off at school and then come to church, picking them up in the afternoon and taking them home. There was only one remaining issue that John had not brought out into the open. He knew there was only one person he could talk to about what was troubling him.

11

Friday 10 am

Robert was still in the hospital when John went to visit him. He had developed a post-operative infection and needed to be on intravenous antibiotics. With any luck it would clear up in a day or so and he could return home. He had been in the hospital for over a week and was getting restless at the confinement, though he wouldn't be able to do much at home for a time. John told him about Mrs. Banks coming to live with them and the surprise at being named the guardians of Jerry and Robin's children. Robert found it all highly entertaining.

"Do you think that Mr. Banks will divorce her?"

"I doubt it. If he divorces her he loses the last possibility of control. In his mind he probably thinks she will come to her senses and go back to him. Plus, think how mad God would be at him if he divorced his wife."

John smiled when he spoke, but Robert quickly tempered his attempt at humor.

"It's really not funny. He's lived by these rules all his life thinking he was doing what was right. He doesn't know any other way to live and he's going to be even more isolated and angry because he thinks he's the only one who's doing what God wants. You haven't heard the last from him, that's for sure. As much as he dislikes you, he'll want you to know how you have wronged him by taking his wife."

"Hey, she's the one who made the choice to leave. I think once she realized she was better and that she could come live with us, that was it."

"But I'm sure he thinks the reason she's better is that he prayed for her. In his mind she owes her life to him because he prayed for her to be healed."

"You don't actually think that God healed her because he prayed for her?"

"You mean why would God answer the prayer of a person like Mr. Banks?"

John thought about what Robert said. He knew that few people came to God with completely pure character and motives, but Mr. Banks? Robert continued,

"Despite what you believe about him, he tries to do what he believes God wants. I know that his approach to God is based on a misunderstanding of his relationship with God, but it's all he knows. You should have some compassion for him. He is consumed by fear, and has probably never known any real assurance that God loves him."

John knew what Robert said was true, but he was bothered by another fact that he could not escape.

"Robert, he has the same Bible that you and I do. He can see the same truths about God that I can. They're right there on the page. I'm not as inclined as you are to give him a pass, especially considering the way he's treated his family over the years."

"I'm not talking about giving him a pass, I'm just trying to help you see why he acts the way he does. You have to understand he doesn't look at the Bible the same way you do. He sees anger where you see acceptance. He sees rules where you see freedom. He sees obedience as the key to life where you see love and gratitude. He relies on tradition to guide him and is fearful of change. You don't have any traditions and are open to new ways to minister to people.

Both of you appeal to the Bible yet both of you are completely opposed to what the other is doing. And it seems that God has used both of you to heal people who were going to die. Kind of makes you think."

John was thinking, but not about Mr. Banks. He had come to the hospital with one last question for Robert, one he knew there might not be an answer for, but one he needed to express to someone. Before he could ask Robert, there was one more thought that Robert wanted to express.

"There is one difference between you two that is obvious when you think about it. From what you have told me, I doubt Mr. Banks has ever experienced any real happiness in his life. I doubt, though, that you'll ever have a chance to talk with him about any of this again. Probably for the best if you ask me."

"Robert, I understand everything you've said about him, it's just that I've lived in the shadow of his legalism for a long time and I'm just beginning to see how it has affected Sharon, much less Mrs. Banks. I can deal with him, but that's not my biggest issue right now."

Robert let the conversation pause in order to let John collect his thoughts. There could be any number of things bothering him, Robert thought. It had only been a week since the accident and Robert had no doubt John was still recovering from the shock. Finally, John began to talk.

"This all started because I prayed for Jerry to be healed. You were right when you told me last week that I was looking for God to do something, anything. I prayed for any number of things for so long without any answer that I was becoming discouraged, though I didn't know it. Then when Jerry was healed it didn't turn out the way I expected, especially personally. It didn't jumpstart my faith and it didn't rejuvenate my spiritual life. In fact, it brought a bunch of problems that made life more difficult. And when they died, I wanted to run away from everything."

He paused as he considered how to say what was on his mind. John didn't want to be misunderstood, so he took a few breaths, and then continued.

"I don't understand everything, but I now believe that something good can come out of this. And now I know what that good is."

Robert also knew what John knew, that the good God intended to come from the tragedy was that God finally answered John's prayer for children. Robert would try to give an answer to a question that John hadn't asked, but he knew was at the front of Johns' mind.

"It doesn't seem fair, does it? You benefitting from a tragedy like this. But I want you to think about this. I believe there are reasons why things happen. Whether you want to believe that God causes everything to happen, or allows everything to happen or things just happen because the world is broken; it really doesn't matter to me. I do know God could prevent tragedies, so if he doesn't there must be a reason. I found this verse in Isaiah 57:1 years ago that I think means if people die before their time, God is saving them from something they might not be able to handle in this life. I don't know what the future might have held for Jerry and Robin, but I believe God always does what's best for his children. For what it's worth, that's what I think."

John listened while Robert spoke, and what he said made sense on one level. But Robert was assuming something that John wasn't. So John finally told someone what he had been thinking for a week, a thought that troubled him more than anything else in the time since the accident. It was always right there, sitting in his subconscious, waiting to come out into the light. He had not brought it up to Amy because he was overwhelmed with everything else swirling around him. Now he was ready, and he said,

"But I don't know that Jerry was a Christian. How was dying in a car accident of any benefit to him if he wasn't going to heaven with his wife?"

It was a big question, and though Robert had personally dealt with it before and found an answer that satisfied him, he waited a moment before sharing it with John.

"Well, for one thing, that's not your concern. That's not what you want to hear, but it's true. If I heard you correctly, he did understand that it was God who healed him. That's an expression of faith, no matter what you might think. I know he didn't bow his head and say a prayer to ask Jesus into his heart, but my guess is he understood where he was with God. I'm not saying that to make you feel good, I'm just talking out loud about how people sometimes believe in ways that aren't what we would call traditional. One last thing. Don't you suppose that if God answered your prayer to heal Jerry, he would answer your prayer for him to be saved as well?"

Robert had one more thing to say to John, but he wanted to give John time to think about what he had just said. After waiting a moment, he said,

"The bottom line is still the same. You can trust God without understanding everything, or you can walk away with your doubts. There have been times when I wanted to walk away. Especially after watching my wife suffering and then die over several years. John, there wasn't anywhere else for me to go."

It was all true, but it didn't bring him the closure he thought he needed. In time he would learn that closure, at least for him, was a myth. He could get past it, but he could not get over it. He would learn to function with doubts and feelings that would surface on occasion to trouble and confuse him. But they were just that, doubts, not certainties, and he would come to understand that God was bigger than his doubts and confusion. John looked at his watch, stood up, and said,

"I'll come and see you when you they let you go home. Right now I have to get back to my kids."

Epilogue

John sat as usual in the front row of the auditorium, waiting for the last song to end. He was thinking about what he would say to the congregation sitting in back of him. They filled the room almost to capacity. It had been a year since he asked people to stay after the service if they wanted him to pray for healing. It had been a long time since he asked people to stay after the service, though the thought occasionally crossed his mind. God was still at work in the church, but the time of healing seemed to have passed. Sitting in the service were a number of people who had been healed during those months. Many had since joined the church and become members.

The song ended, and as the worship team exited the stage John walked to the podium and began to speak. He spoke without notes, because what he wanted to say was part of him. He didn't need words on a page to remind him of the year's events. He knew most of the faces, but new people visited every Sunday. One face in particular, sitting toward the back, drew his attention. He looked at her for a moment before he began to speak.

"A year ago we had a visitor in our service. He is here every week but sometimes we don't notice him. Some of you were visiting that Sunday. It may have been the first time you had ever attended a church, and you were apprehensive about what we would do. You came that morning because you heard that God healed a man of terminal cancer. This man was literally at death's door. You either saw his story on TV or read about it in the newspaper. You came because you had nothing to lose. You came because you thought something good could happen to you.

"Not everyone who came that Sunday morning was healed. Some, but not all. Why, I still can't tell you even though I have spent a lot of time in the last year thinking about what happened that morning and in the days that followed. Those of you who were members of this church were perhaps caught off guard by what happened that morning, just as I was. God decided to show up in a different manner than we had ever experienced, and for some of you it was way out of your comfort zone. But I want to commend those of you who stayed. It can be difficult to experience your faith in a new ways. You saw God work in ways our church had not seen before.

"Most of you also know that the man who was healed, and his wife, died in a car accident just a week later."

John paused for a moment to collect himself. Though it had been a year, the memory of those events were still fresh in his mind. The room was completely still as he looked down at the podium. He had not told anyone he was going to speak of those events, so the crowd was unusually attentive. He raised his head and continued,

"Many of you know that I was thrown for a loop when Jerry and Robin died. I did and said things that showed my confusion and doubt. I could not explain to myself, or to anyone else, why God would heal a man one day and then seven days later that same man would die, along with his wife.

"I know God understands what I was going through. He is patient, kind and understanding. That confusion didn't last very long, but it was real, and it was very painful. I also learned things about myself during that time, but more importantly I learned things about God. Things that I may have understood in my mind, but not experienced in my heart.

"I learned that I was not as strong as I thought I was. But I also learned that God is stronger than I had ever thought.

"I learned that it's okay to ask questions. It's okay to get upset when things happen that we don't understand. But I also learned that God is big enough. He's not upset with my questions or my anger.

"I learned that what I think is best is seldom what's really the best, either for me or for someone else. I came to understand that God knows what's best, though it may take months or years to come to that understanding.

"I also learned a lot about prayer. I was looking for God to answer my prayers. I thought it would prove that he was there and involved in my life. I learned, not easily, that he's there all the time, no matter how he answers my prayers.

"I learned that "no" is an acceptable answer to my prayers. So is "wait". I think that God says "no" and "wait" more than "yes" because he wants me to love him for who he is, not for what he can do.

"Finally, I learned to expect the unexpected when I pray. When he does answer our prayers, it may not be in the way we expect, though I believe it will always be for our good."

John spoke for a few more minutes, and then asked the worship team back to the stage to close the service with a final song. As he returned to his seat in the first row, he again looked at the young woman sitting toward the back. For a moment their eyes met. He sat down and knew what he needed to do, though he was not without some doubt.

She stood in a corner of the lobby as John spoke to people who sought him out. He wasn't worried about her leaving; he knew she would wait until he was available to talk with her.

He heard them before he saw them. Their high pitched voices had become part of his life in the last year. He turned to see them run into the lobby from the hall that came from their Sunday school class. Sharon, who taught their class, was right behind them. She stopped to talk to Edward, and John noticed that she was just beginning to show. They would have to think about telling people soon. When the girls saw John they ran to him and excitedly showed him the crafts they had made that morning. John bent down and examined the creations as if they were treasures, taking time to compliment them on their artwork. Realizing that it was time to speak to the young woman, he said to the girls,

"Go show Edward what you've made. Daddy has to talk to someone. Then we'll go out to lunch with mom."

He straightened up and walked over to her. She was nervous and was holding her purse across her chest in a protective manner. He smiled, extended his hand, and then said,

"I'm glad you came today. You have something you need me to pray for, so why don't we go back into the auditorium and talk."

Made in the USA
San Bernardino, CA
04 December 2018